MW00624891

Gardening Month by Month:

Tips for Flowers, Vegetables, Lawns, & Houseplants

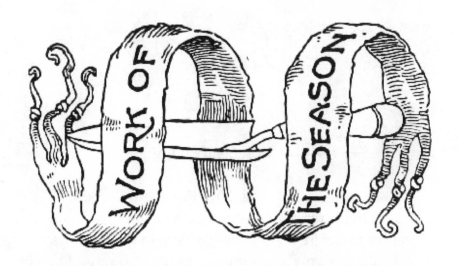

Easy-Growing Gardening Guide, Vol. 11

Rosefiend Cordell

Rosefiend Publishing

Copyright © 2017 Rosefiend Cordell
All rights reserved. Although the author has made every effort to ensure that the information in this book was correct at press time, the author does not assume and hereby disclaims any liability to any party for any loss, damage, or disruption caused by errors or omissions, whether such errors or omissions result from negligence, accident, raspberry shortages, burned toast, totalitarian rule, sweating to death after the air-conditioning goes out, missed deadlines, man-eating groundhogs, being unable to find a good pair of reading glasses, presbyopia, dry rot, treason, butts (cigarette and others), stag beetles, or any other reason.

DEDICATION

To Brad

I consider myself
the luckiest gal
on the face of the earth.

Contents

January

Save Time and Trouble With Garden Journals

When I worked as a horticulturist taking care of twelve high-maintenance gardens over seven square miles of city, as well as several hundred small trees, a greenhouse, and whatever else the bosses threw at me, I had to find a way to keep organized besides waking up at 3 a.m. to make extensive lists. My solution: keep an extensive garden journal.

Vegetable gardeners with an organized journal can take control of production and yields (or, if they have ornamentals, make everything look even lovelier). When you have a large garden or a small organic farm, you must keep track of everything in order to beat the pests, make the most of your harvest, or keep the colors in the perennial garden matched.

Keeping a garden journal reduces stress because your overtaxed brain won't have to carry around all those lists, and it saves time by keeping you focused. Writing sharpens the mind, helps it to retain more information, and opens your eyes to the world around you.

My journal is a 9.5 x 6 five-section notebook, college ruled, and I leave it open to the page I'm working on at the time. The only drawback with a spiral notebook is that after a season or two I have to thumb through a lot of pages to find an earlier comment. A small three-ring binder with five separators would do the trick, too – if you wish, you can take out pages at the end of each season and file them in a master notebook.

I keep two notebooks – one for ornamentals and one for vegetables. However, you might prefer to pile everything into one notebook. Do what feels comfortable to you.

Here are the five sections I divide my notebooks into – though you might use different classifications, or put them in different orders. Don't sweat it; this ain't brain surgery. Experiment a little. You'll eventually settle into the form that suits you best.

First section: To-do lists.

This is pretty self-explanatory: you write a list, you cross off almost everything on it, you make a new list.

When I worked as horticulturist, I did these lists monthly. I'd visit all the gardens I took care of. After looking at anything left unfinished on the previous month's list, and looking at the garden to see what else needed to be done, I made a new, comprehensive list.

Use one page of the to-do section for reminders of things you need to do next season. If it's summer, and you think of some chores you'll need to do this fall, make a FALL page and write them down. Doing this has saved me lots of headaches.

Second section: Reference lists.

These are lists that you'll refer back to on occasion.

For example, I'd keep a list of all the yews in the parks system that needed trimmed, a list of all gardens that needed weekly waterings, a list of all places that needed sprayed for bagworms, a list of all the roses that needed to be babied, etc.

I would also keep my running lists in this section, too – lists I keep adding to.

For instance, I kept a list of which flowers were in bloom – even flowers I didn't own, including trees and shrubs. Then when I made a landscape plan, I would look at the bloom list to get sure-fire combinations, and I could also be certain that I could maintain year-round color.

You can also keep a wish list – plants and vegetables you'd like to have in your garden.

Third section: Tracking progress.

This will also be a weekly (or, "whenever it occurs to me to write about it") section as well.

If you have a greenhouse, keep track of what seeds you order, when you plant them, when they germinate, how many plants you transplant (and how many survive to maturity), and so forth.

At the end of the greenhouse season, use these pages to look back and record your thoughts – "I will never again try to start vinca from seeds! Never!! Never!!!" Then you don't annoy yourself by doing these things next year.

Do the same thing when you move on to the vegetable garden – when you tilled the ground, planted the seeds, when they germinated, and so forth. Make notes on yields and how everything tasted. "The yellow crooknecks were definitely not what I'd hoped for. Try yellow zucchini next year."

Be sure to write a vegetable garden overview at season's end, too. "Next year, for goodness' sake, get some 8-foot poles for the beans! Also, drive the poles deeper into the ground so they don't fall over during thunderstorms." And so forth.

During the winter, you can look back on this section and see ways you can improve your yields and harvest ("The dehydrator worked great on the tomatoes!"), and you can see which of your experiments worked.

Fourth section: Details of the natural world.

When keeping a journal, don't limit yourself to what's going on in your garden. Track events in the natural world, too. Write down when the poplars start shedding cotton or when the Queen's Anne Lace blooms.

You've heard old gardening maxims such as "plant corn when oak leaves are the size of a squirrel's ear," or "prune roses when the forsythia blooms." If the spring has been especially cold and everything's behind, you can rely on nature's cues instead of a calendar when planting or preventing disease outbreaks.

Also, by setting down specific events, you can look at the journal later and say, "Oh, I can expect little caterpillars to attack the indigo plant when the Johnson's Blue geranium is blooming." Then next year, before the geranium blooms, you can seek out the caterpillar eggs and squish them before they hatch. An ounce of prevention, see?

When I read back over this section of the journal, patterns start to emerge. I noticed that Stargazer lilies bloom just as the major heat begins. This is no mere coincidence: It's happened for the last three years! So now when I see the large buds, I give the air conditioner a quick checkup.

Fifth section: Notes and comments.

This is more like the journal that most people think of as being a journal – here, you just talk about the garden, mull over how things are looking, or grouse at that Redgold rose for becoming blackspot-on-a-stick.

I generally put a date on each entry, then ramble on about any old thing. You can write a description of the garden at sunset, sketch your coneflowers, or keep track of the habits of bugs you see crawling around in the plants. This ain't art, this is just fun stuff (which, in the end, yields great dividends).

Maybe you've been to a seminar on the habits of Asian melons and you need a place to put your notes. Put them here!

This would be a good place to put garden plans, too. Years later I run into them again, see old mistakes I've made, and remember neat combinations that I haven't tried yet.

Then, get a calendar.

When winter comes, get next year's calendar and the gardening journal and sit down at the kitchen table. Using last year's notes, mark on the calendar events to watch out for -- when the tomatoes first ripen, when the summer heat starts to break, and when you expect certain insects to attack. In the upcoming year, you just look at the calendar and say, "Well, the squash bugs will be hatching soon," so you put on your garden gloves and start smashing the little rafts of red eggs on the plants.

A garden journal can be a fount of information, a source of memories, and most of all, a way to keep organized. Who thought a little spiral notebook could do so much?

New Year's Resolutions

Wow, is it the new year already? Time for a couple of new year's resolutions for the garden and yard.

* You know what the biggest resolution should be? To go organic.

Chemical companies really have us in a headlock, because so many people think that every gardening problem can be solved by spraying something. This is an approach that does more harm than good. We use chemical fertilizers to "feed" plants instead of replenishing the soil with organic matter. With organic material, the plant can choose the nutrients it needs, and the nutrients are in a form that's more readily taken up by the roots. Organic material also benefits the myriad creatures that live below the ground. Just because we can't see the bacteria, protozoans, or tiny insects that work there doesn't mean they don't exist. And when these creatures go to work, the soil becomes more hospitable to plants.

Earthworms are among the biggest workhorses of the soil, and they love organic stuff. Earthworm castings are great fertilizer, bringing nutrients to the earth's surface from deep in the subsoil. Earthworm burrows bring air deep into the ground. Plant roots clump around their burrows for the nutrients the earthworms secrete as they crawl along. They mix the organic matter into the soil. Throw away your tiller and let worms till the soil for you.

* Resolve to act in plant-positive ways instead of pest-negative ways. That is, resolve to concentrate on making your plants happy and strong so they can resist diseases, instead of acting only when pests or diseases appear.

Plants are like people – if you eat right and exercise, then you have a better shot at fighting off diseases, especially the long-term ones like diabetes and heart disease. Of course this doesn't mean loading your African violet onto the treadmill; instead, you look for ways to keep the plant healthy, happy, and strong. Pests and diseases prey on plants that are stressed.

So, put your plant where it will be happiest, and start on the next resolution:

* Resolve to fix the soil. Once your plant is in the ground, it's stuck there for good unless you decide to move it. The soil that's around the roots is the soil your plant has to live with, and if it's lousy soil, it is not going to be a happy plant.

And fixing the soil is a plant-positive thing to do. So pile on the leafmould and compost, add greensand (which is a rock powder that's high in potassium and iron), compost some manure and put it on. Bone and blood meal are great. When your plants come up, mulch them with newspapers and grass clippings.

After you go fishing, bury the fish scraps deeply by the corn. Put coffee grounds and tea bags by acid-loving plants. Make a compost pile where you pile on weeds, algae, fresh manure, leaves, alfalfa hay, fruit and vegetable scraps, bread heels, hair, etc. If you have a compost pile that's slow to break down, get some red wiggler worms and add them in. Red wigglers will turn your pile into some wonderful soil, and you also get a lot of earthworm castings. Just keep the pile watered so it stays moist, not wet, so the worms can do their work. (Don't use nightcrawlers, because crawlers prefer to live deep in the soil, while wigglers live in leaf litter.)

Just a few resolutions to make your garden and plants happier and healthier.

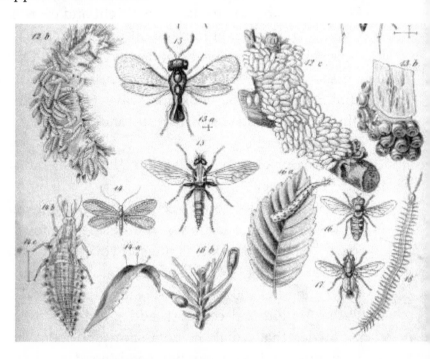

Garden Catalog Mayhem!

This time of year, I want to get the garden organized. I sent off for a zillion seed catalogues last month, so they should start clogging the mailbox any day now.

My Seed Savers Exchange catalogue (www.seedsavers.org) has already shown up. I am so in love with their pictures of heirloom vegetables. I wish I could plant all of them, except there's only so much room in the garden. The "Tigger" melons are cute, all red-orange zigzags on a little yellow globe, and they are fragrant. "Queen Anne's Pocket Melon" has small, orange fruits with a powerful fragrance, though the white flesh is rather bland. The catalogue says that women used to carry these in their pockets for the perfume. But I'm probably going to get the yellow Asian melon, "Sakata's Sweet." This has baseball-sized, yellow melons with sweet flesh, and it can be trellised. (I need a small melon because I might be the only person in my household who eats it.)

I'm no fan of peppers – the only thing I use them for is soup seasoning. Also, I can't handle anything spicier than Taco Bell mild sauce. This "Fish" pepper they offer is about medium heat (which means it would make me spit flames), but I am tempted to get a few seeds anyway. It's an African-American heirloom with variegated leaves. The peppers have the most amazing blends of green, red, orange, and yellow.

The only peppers I'm going to get are small, colorful ones with a heat rating of zero. "Tequila Sunrise" has orange, carrot-shaped fruits. The miniature bells (chocolate, red, and yellow) are cute. "Healthy" has carrot-shaped red fruits. I'll probably have to flip a coin with these.

I'm going to get fingerling potatoes, I think. These are the small, skinny potatoes that are a gourmet's delight. Problem is, they're priced for gourmets, too. Most of them cost $12.50 for a 2 ½ pound bag. I should just bite the bullet and get them.

Do you want a taste sample of your potatoes before you buy them? Wood Prairie Farm in Bridgewater, Maine (www.woodprairie.com), offers a Potato of the Month Club, where they send you three potato varieties every month in a ten-pound gift box, from September to April. You can also order fresh organic vegetables – roots like shallots, "Chantenay" carrots, parsnips, and so forth – through the winter. Wood Prairie Farm and Seed Savers Exchange also offer packages of dried beans. So you *can* "taste and try before you buy."

I've got to get into the garden and start figuring out where everything will go. In my garden, this will make for an interesting (read: haphazard) plan, since I will grow two tomato plants, one pepper plant, one tepee of pole beans, one melon, two summer squash, etc.. I'm going to be sharing an awful lot of seeds this year. Also, when one crop (like lettuce) finishes up, I throw another crop or flower in to fill in the area, adding to the randomness of the garden. But I'm not growing for show. I'm interested in production!

Heirloom Vegetables – History Plus Taste Plus Hardiness

Anybody who has enjoyed tasty vegetables in their garden can find even greater taste, variety, and color through heirloom vegetables – some of which have been around for generations, and even farther back to the earliest days of mankind!

Heirloom vegetables grow true to seed – that is, if you plant a seed from an heirloom, you will get the exact same plant – unlike hybrid vegetables. So when you pick an heirloom tomato, you are picking the same kind of tomato that your great-great-great grandma might have picked in her garden.

History is part of the allure. Many of these heirlooms have a long pedigree. Thomas Jefferson, the third President of the United States, sought out many fruits and vegetables from all over the world to grow at Monticello, which are still grown there today – varieties that are over 200 years old. You can grow the same vegetables that one of our nation's founders enjoyed! Not bad!

And the sheer variety of heirloom seeds is mind-boggling. If you look at the tomatoes in the Bakers Creek Seed Company catalog, you are in for a treat. I had no ideas that we have white tomatoes! Or purple carrots, or even yellow ones! Dainty little white eggplants that really look like eggs! Weird stretchy purple eggplant, and varieties in orange and yellow … potatoes in all hues and sizes … lettuces with pretty red speckles … and beans that have been around since early humans lived in the Fertile Crescent. Yellow and orange melons from Asia. In December and January, these heirloom seed catalogs are both a delight and a bane – a bane because you want to try every single one of these plants, but eventually you will have to make actual choices and weed down your huge list to a measly few. The pain is real, people.

Hybrids – hybridized plants – are the result of a cross between two plant varieties. Let's say a grower has two tomatoes, each with a different trait that he wants to combine into one plant. So, the grower crosses these two tomatoes and gets a plant that has both traits. (Technically, when you are trying to create a new variety, the process is much more complicated, and involves a long process of growing every seed from the hybridized plant, putting the fruit and plants through trials in which the lousy plants and bad-tasting fruit that result from this cross are discarded while the good ones are tested and grown, until the breeder finds a strong, sturdy plant that also bears good fruits that seems to be worth marketing … anyway it takes a long time to hybridize a new variety, and then the subsequent marketing also takes time. End digression.)

Now, if you plant the seeds from this hybridized fruit, they will revert back to one of the parents.

Hybrids are nice, but there's one difference: Heirlooms are open-pollinated plants – that is, it doesn't matter how they're pollinated, but the seeds will always grow into the same plant, generation after generation. Hybrids can't.

Another good reason to raise heirlooms is flavor. Many commercial varieties of vegetables grown today are not grown for flavor but in order to bear fruit that ships well. Let me repeat that: The vegetables aren't chosen because they taste good – they're chosen because they can travel well for hundreds of miles!

Now, obviously if you're going to just pick a couple of tomatoes and carry them in through the back door, you really don't need this requirement. You just want something you can stick in your mouth and start chomping on, and you want to have a big smile on your face when you do. Heirlooms definitely fit the bill.

A lot of heirloom varieties have been lost over the years. In the early 1900s, this country had nearly 7,000 varieties of apples in commerce. These days, that number stands at less than a thousand. The same goes for our garden fruits and vegetables. The movement toward heirlooms is an attempt to bring those numbers back up – to keep the gene pool for these different plants as wide and diverse as possible – and to bring back some of that history we've lost. And also, because this stuff is just flat-out fun to grow. People meeting some of these colorful heirloom tomatoes for the first time are like kids with a box of crayons, checking out all the cool colors.

Heirlooms – A cool way to enjoy history.

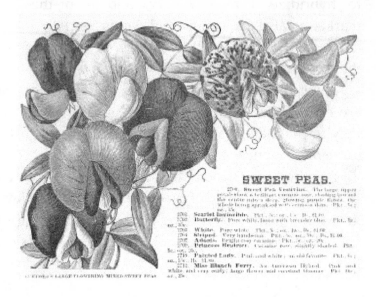

January To-Do List

January is such a slow month, but there are still things you can do to keep yourself occupied and get ready for spring.

- Check your tools to be sure everything is sharpened and oiled. You might be surprised by rust on some tools if they were improperly put away last fall. It's better to be surprised now than in early spring. Rub the wooden handles of your tools with paraffin. Check the tire on your wheelbarrow to see if it needs aired or replaced. You might even give the wheelbarrow a fresh coat of paint if it's starting to get rust spots.
- Once the weather warms up, spray horticultural oil on your fruit trees, raspberry canes, and roses (if the roses aren't completely covered up). These will also benefit from a dose of lime sulfur, at winter strength, once a month. Studies

have shown that roses sprayed with lime sulfur through the winter have less disease through the year.

Of course, being able to spray when the weather is halfway decent is a challenge. "Hey, boss, I'm going home the rest of the day to spray my roses, bye!" Not in our lifetime.

Also, prune your fruit trees for the upcoming season.

• Add more mulch to your plants if necessary. Do you have leaf piles from last fall that are still out of control? Run the lawn mower over the leaves to chop them and use them as mulch. I got ten big bags of leaves from my grandma, and about seven bags from my neighbors, spread them all over the garden, then mowed and mowed. It took about an hour, but the big heaps of leaves became a good layer of mulch.

Now I wish I had more leaves. The ground under the leaf mulch doesn't freeze as brick-solid as unmulched ground, and you can see that the earthworms have been busy under the leaves – and the more earthworms you have, the healthier your soil is.

• Water your outside plants, which lose moisture through their stems and their buds. Of course, do this when the temps are above 32 degrees!

• Wash your pots and trays to get ready for seeding plants next month. Use hot, soapy water, then rinse with a mild bleach solution and let them dry.

• Set up a cold frame. I'm making mine simple – a couple of bales of alfalfa hay against the side of the house with an old storm window on top. I probably could make a simple box with scrap lumber, but, to quote Pig from the Kipper cartoons that my daughter likes to watch, "Oh, I'm not at all clever like that." (You know you're a mom when you can quote cartoons just as well as your child.)

Once the cold frame is set up and has warmed the ground underneath it, mix some potting soil into the ground and sow lettuce, spinach, carrots, radishes, and salad greens. You might have mixed success with the root vegetables, but it never hurts to try.

Keep a thermometer inside the cold frame, and one outside. Open the cold frame a crack when daytime temperatures rise over 40 degrees, and wider when temps hit 60 degrees. Of course, be sure to close the cold frame at night.

• You can still plant spring-flowering bulbs any time when the ground is not frozen. They might not bloom this year, but they'll have forgiven you by next year (if the voles haven't eaten them by then).

January Garden Checklist for Zones 7 to 9

For folks who live way on south where it's warm over the winter....

Zone 7

Clean out your cold frame.

Start your perennial, cole crop, and annual seeds indoors.

Plant shrubs and trees. Bare-root roses (or any other bare-root shrub or tree) can be planted now if the ground is not wet.

Bare-root perennial vegetables (asparagus, strawberries, etc.) can also be planted now.

Spray dormant (or horticultural) oil on fruit trees *before* buds swell.

Fruit trees that have had canker problems in the past need to be sprayed.

If you didn't plant your bulbs last fall, you might as well do it now. They probably won't bloom this spring, but they should be fine next year.

Clean out the gardens where needed and see where you need a little more mulch. Get the garden ready to go now, before all the spring chaos breaks loose!

Zone 8

If you've started cabbages, broccoli, or other cole crops, start hardening them off outside – get them used to the outside conditions before you transplant them.

Spout seed potatoes by setting them in a bright place.

Spray dormant (or horticultural) oil on fruit trees or any shrub infected with scale.

Sow peas, lettuce, and other early crops outside at the end of the month.

Divide and replant crowded perennials or bulbs.

Plant trees, shrubs, and bare-root roses now.

Start sowing seeds indoors for annuals and perennials.

When winter-blooming trees have finished flowering, prune them back lightly.

Plant bare-root perennial vegetables (strawberries, asparagus, etc.).

Sow cold-season crops such as peas, spinach, and lettuce.

Have sheets ready to throw over tender plants during frost.

Zone 9

Sow beets, carrots, peas, lettuce, and other early crops directly in the garden.

Start seeds of tomatoes, peppers, and eggplants inside. Watch out for damping-off disease. You can also start warm-season flowers such as petunias, begonias, and impatiens in early January. Start marigolds and periwinkles in late January.

Plant persimmons, loquats, and figs. Plant young pistachios and stake them securely.

Plant summer-blooming bulbs.

Plant citrus trees.

Plant seedlings of cool-season and winter vegetables.

Plant bulbs such as gladiolus and dahlias now.

Cut back roses in February, and clean out dead canes. On climbing roses, don't prune now, but use this time to train them to where you want them to go. Don't prune the once-blooming shrub roses or climbing roses until after they bloom.

February

Birds of Missouri

A few days ago, when it was snowing and the wind was rocking the barren, black trees, I looked out the window and saw a flock of robins sitting in the road. The road at least was bare of snow, and offered a few puddles, out of which one robin was drinking. The rest of the flock sat around with the wind ruffling their feathers, probably wondering what possessed them to return so soon.

A little after that, I saw an eastern bluebird sitting on the roof of my neighbor's house. I guess spring will be on its way, eventually.

Speaking of birds, the Missouri Department of Conversation has a bird book out. And it's about time – they have published guide books for every other kind of creature –flowers, orchids, fish, even amphibians and reptiles, for you herpetologists out there.

The book, *Birds of Missouri* by Brad Jacobs, lists and gives pictures of 354 of the 398 known bird species that have been seen in Missouri. The book lists habitat types specific to each bird, such as urban areas, tallgrass prairies, upland and second growth forests, and so forth.

Each bird in the book has a picture and a short description, as well as a notation as to what habitat(s) they can be found in, as well as other information. On each page, there is also a sidebar about some interesting piece of information about the bird or birds listed on that page, such as where wild turkeys roost, how to tell a crane from a heron, unusual hummingbird varieties to look for, or the difference between the possibly-extinct Ivory-billed woodpecker and the Pileated woodpecker, which can be seen in some places in the state.

Maps are also included to show the species' range through the state, and what months the birds can be seen. You need to look at the key in the front of the book to understand how to read them, however.

In the back of the books are the listings of rare or irregular winter visitors, regular but rare birds, and types of birds that might get blown in by the occasional hurricane. There is also information about bird watching, bird surveys, how to report bird sightings and where to report them. Birds are also listed by family in the back, so you can see which birds are related. I was surprised to see that the coot is in the same family as the Sandhill crane. (If you've never seen a coot, it's like a little duck with huge weird feet.)

The book is good for browsing or just reading through at random. The birds seem to be grouped by families, though this isn't always obvious (the coot and the Sandhill crane are on the same page, for instance, but they are in the same family) – perhaps later editions could list families and orders somewhere on the page.

The book runs 375 pages long and costs $30, and is available at any Missouri Department of Conversation service center. Or, go online at http://www.mdcnatureshop.com/ and click on "Books." You can also call down to Jefferson City to order the book at (573) 751-4115. Don't forget that Heritage Card discount that's available!

available as alternate
ve as the hibernating
les, which feed more or
mer periods of winter.
can be found feeding,
at of the District of
ary, "even after heavy
again in March.

ON APHIS BY NATURAL
EMIES.

rol of this pest with
natural enemies, aided

Write Your Shopping Lists for Spring!

I got my seeds a month ago. They aren't doing much in the bag, and it's way too early to plant, but I just like to take them out and look at them once in a while. Then my daughter takes the bean seeds and goes around the house shaking them like maracas, and I have to put them away. I like to imagine what the garden might yield, though the little pessimist that lives in my mind keeps bringing to my daydreams images of blight and drought and cats leaving smelly presents in the mulch.

Undeterred by my inner cynic, I've started making my supply list. First, a little gallon sprayer and a half-pint of insecticidal soap concentrate. That's for any bug infestations that might start eating my crops. Squash bugs sound particularly nasty. You can use insecticidal soap right up to the day before harvest with no adverse effects, though I'd still wash the soapy taste off the vegetables. It's non-toxic, too. However, some plants don't take too well to insecticidal soap, like impatiens. Check the label before you buy.

Neem oil is also a good, non-toxic insecticide that's becoming more common, as is pyrethrin, which is extracted from a type of daisy. Do not get pyrethrins mixed up with pyrethroids, which is the synthetic form of the poison. (Whatever you plan to spray, always read and follow label direction. More insecticide is not better, it is simply more – and the extra heads right into our groundwater supply.)

I'm considering getting floating row covers. These can be a valuable asset in the garden. They let sun and rain in, but can keep a light frost at bay. They also keep invading insects out. So, when you put your vegetable plants in the ground, cover them to keep squash bugs and flea beetles away. (You'll still have to deal with cutworms, which come up through the soil.) When the flowers appear you'll have to uncover them so bees can get in to pollinate them.

I still need to bring home three pallets. I'm going to wire them together, set them next to the garden, and move my compost pile into it. The compost heap would be more handy there than clear across the yard. I'd also like it close to the back door so I can lean outside and throw eggshells and apple cores into it.

To nourish the ground I'll grab some bone meal, some blood meal, and some Bradfield fertilizer, which is all-natural and contains alfalfa. Alfalfa releases a chemical called tricontanol, which gives plants a growth boost. Oh, yeah, don't forget the compost.

Don't leave the bone meal or blood meal unattended outside because dogs and cats will eat it.

For cats that leave presents in the mulch ... I'm thinking about planting catnip at the far end of the yard as a trap crop, hoping that might divert their attention, BUT you know how well that's going to work. What might work better would be to invest in three small Super-Soaker water guns, one for each window that looks over the garden. Anytime I glimpse a cat sniffing around the mulch, I'll stealthily raise the window and *fire*!

It might be as ineffective as the catnip patch, but it would be a lot more fun.

March

Square Foot Gardening

I picked up a copy of *Square Foot Gardening* by Mel Bartholomew for five bucks on the Internet, because I was having a heck of a time planning my vegetable garden. I don't need a whole lot of plants in the vegetable garden, so planting a million rows didn't make any sense. Two yellow squash plants are more than enough, for instance. Then the book arrived in the mail, and I found the system I'd been looking for. It's simple, and it's not wasteful.

First, the simple part. The backbone of the garden is the one-foot squares. You take four of these one-foot squares and put them together in a kind of grid. Separating these squares are paths, about one foot square, so you don't walk on the soil inside the four-foot areas.

When you make the garden plan, you'll be drawing a lot of "windows," like the windows a little kid would draw on a picture of a house. In each "pane" you're growing one crop. For example:

Basil	Tomato
16 Beets	Flowers

Spacing is pretty straightforward. In each one-foot square you can plant one, four, nine, or 16 plants, depending on their normal space requirements. So, there would be only one tomato, pepper, eggplant, or potato plant per square. Chard, bush beans, herbs, and large lettuce could be planted four per square. Other lettuces could be planted nine per square. Root crops like carrots, radishes, and beets could be planted 16 per square. Then zucchini gets its own special category – it will take three feet of the four-foot square, and in the remaining area you could plant root vegetables or lettuce, plants that you'll have already harvested by the time the greedy zucchini sprawls all over.

Spacing isn't set in stone, of course. If you want to grow a monster tomato plant that feeds the world, then set it in the middle of a four-foot square and get out of the way.

Plants like cantaloupe, pole beans, peas, and cucumbers are grown on trellises, which saves space, and also saves you from stooping over and hunting for the vegetables.

Next, the frugal part. You plant *only as many seeds as you need*. Instead of dumping 2,000 lettuce seeds in the ground, you plant nine, or 16. Honestly, do you really intend to eat 2,000 lettuces? And as for thinning: isn't it silly to grow all those seedlings, then pull up half of them? More often, you forget to thin the seedlings, then you end up with plants crowded together like sardines. They never reach their full size, so your crop is nowhere as good as it might have been.

So plant only as much as you can eat, then give the extra seeds to your friends.

The benefits to square-foot gardening are many. To plan, you draw a bunch of windowpanes until you get something you like, then you scale them to size and slap them on your garden plan. You plant only what you need, which is a manageable amount. No waste! You don't walk all over the garden, just on the paths, and you can reach into the four-foot area and harvest without compacting the soil. Put scrap lumber on the path, or newspapers, or a heavy mulch, and you keep weeds down. There's less work all around – and more time to enjoy gardening.

Getting Ready for Spring Tilling

I always think my spring columns take on a more hectic pace – mainly because there's so much going on at once. You just have to hit the ground running.

If you're planning to till your garden, be sure to do several things.

First, the soil has got to be dry. When you till up wet soil, you're tearing up the soil's structure. Soil that was loose and crumbly will turn into solid clods, or will form a water-repelling crust on the surface.

Before you till the ground, take a handful of soil and squeeze it. If water drips out, forget it! If you open your hand and the clod is still solid, don't till. If you open your hand and the clod falls apart in little crumbles, then grab the tiller and go to work.

Second, before you till, renew the organic matter in the soil. You should do this every year, because soil microorganisms and worms are constantly busy with breaking down the organic matter for your plants. (Actually, tilling burns organic material faster because the air that's incorporated into the soil causes the microorganisms to work faster.) Spread leafmold, compost, rotted manure over the ground and till it in.

If you have a lot of weeds growing on the garden, then till them under, too. When you do that, they become a valuable green manure that will break down and add nutrients to the soil. Just be sure to till them under well so they don't start growing back again.

If you use your weeds as green manure, you will have to delay planting seeds for about a month while you're letting it break down completely. However, if you're just going to skip seed planting and put in the tomato and squash plants in May, then knock yourself out. There's enough time for it to work!

Green manures improve the soil structure, because the decomposing plants add ingredients to the soil that help to bind together soil particles. The result: a more crumbly soil that's easier to till.

Tilling is a good way to prepare the soil for spring. But in some ways it's also bad for the soil. Tilling destroys earthworm burrows, putting a dent in the earthworm population. A healthy soil has a high population of worms, so you could be shooting yourself in the foot. Sometimes soils that are repeatedly tilled form a compacted layer just below the tines. (Soil that's disked or plowed also develops the same problems.)

To avoid this, you might till every other year, or some years double-dig the soil to break up that compacted layer. Also, leaving some areas of the garden untilled (for example, by including a strawberry or asparagus patch inside the garden) will give the worms time to multiply.

You might even leave small portions of the garden fallow, planting alfalfa, clover, or some legume to fix nitrogen for a year. Then next year, till the area under and plant your corn there. Shoot, if the farmers can do it, then why can't we?

If there's no area of your garden that you can leave fallow, then interplant clover among your vegetables. Use clover to cover your garden walkways, or plant white clover between your rows of corn. Legumes will add nitrogen to the soil, bring in beneficial insects, and act as a living mulch through the heat of the summer. While other gardens are withering, your garden is nice and cool with all that green on the ground.

Why Soilbuilding is So Important

I am convinced of the importance of building the soil, whether it's in the vegetable garden, perennial border, the lawn, even farmland. I don't mean using chemical fertilizers. Soil building means you're providing enough organic material to feed the worms and all of the creatures and microorganisms that live down there.

This is the biggest irony of chemical fertilizers: when you use them *without* organic material, you are starving the ground.

Stick with me a moment on this one. In nature, everything returns to the soil: leaves, grass, manure, seed fluff, dead animals. In nature, the soil is filled with activity. Worms eat their way through the soil, bringing air (which is a good fertilizer – all that nitrogen) into the subsoil. Worm castings make soil nutrients readily available to plants. Root hairs seek out the worms' tunnels for the nutrients they can find there.

Bacteria, when breaking down organic material, create polysaccharides that make the soil stick better, thereby improving soil structure.

Many types of fungus help trees and plants collect nutrients and minerals from organic material and the soil. These fungi are called mycorrhizae. Mycorrhizae grow into plant roots and send threads many miles through the soil, which brings the plants all kinds of nutrients they wouldn't normally be able to reach. In return, the fungi get carbohydrates – sugar – from the plants.

Many mushrooms you see – even morels – act as mycorrhizae. And there are many other fungi that you never see above the ground, serving the same function. Scientists still don't know all the types and varieties of fungi that exist.

Trees reach their roots into the subsoil, bringing up nutrients that your average plant can't reach. These nutrients go into the leaves. When the leaves fall and decay, those nutrients are released to the topsoil.

What I'm telling you about the soil is extremely oversimplified. There are millions of things going on in the soil that we don't see happening, and millions of processes and creatures that still baffle scientists. Yet because we don't see it, we assume there's nothing there.

Now look at those barren lawns all over town. People bag up their grass clippings, bag up their leaves, and send all of these riches to the dump. Nothing's going into the soil … except chemicals. So we are destroying these processes, systematically, all over the nation.

Help the soil biomass do its work. Mow the leaves and grass clippings into the yard. (Also, it's a lot less work for you.)

Fifteen big bags of leaves, when chewed up by a lawnmower, turn into an inch of mulch over a 15 by 24' garden. I did that last fall; this spring, I'm finding worm castings all over!

Pour the leaves out on your garden, mow them up, and till them under. Or just leave them on top of the soil and don't bother tilling. Plant your seeds under the mulch, and they'll stay moist and come right up when it's time. With mulch, you don't have to worry about your garden drying out.

The more I read about earthworms and observe them, the more I am convinced that these guys are a blessing to the soil. Give them leaves and let them work.

You don't have leaves? Take a trip to the local landfill and get some. There are leaves all over, free for the taking. (Be careful with grass clippings. Those often contain herbicides that will kill your garden plants.) Or grab them off the curb before the garbage truck arrives.

Spring Wildflowers

As the faint, mistlike green starts showing in the trees and across fields, as flower buds on magnolias and dogwoods grow fat, the first wildflowers will start coming up.

This is a great time to head for the woods (as long as it's not too wet!) and just tramp around in the stillness broken by the singing of cardinals and chickadees.

Look for the early fiddleheads of ferns breaking through the leafmould, for the white Dutchman's breeches (they look like white pantaloons hanging upside down and are related to bleeding-hearts) and for the white harbinger of spring.

Appropriate name, right? About late April, we'll see lady's slippers and putty-root orchids and some showy orchis.

Wildflowers bloom when the trees are still leafless -- when sunlight can reach the forest floor. These are among my favorite plants, because they're the ones I know best. For reading about wildflowers, "Missouri Wildflowers" by Edgar Denison is good reading.

A few years ago, I graduated to "Flora of Missouri" by Julian Steyermark (I just call it Steyermark's). It's 4 inches thick and has everything!

Before I go on, let's go over the most important rule in wildflower enjoyment: please, don't pick!

In his essay, "Wildflower Conservation" in "Missouri Wildflowers," Mr. Denison said, "We have all seen a nosegay of wilted flowers thrown away along a field path, a sight encountered even in parks where picking flowers is specifically prohibited. ... The idea that flowers are there for the picking is a mistaken one. It is one thing to harvest' flowers which have been grown in gardens or nurseries and another when we deal with wildflowers."

And who's to know that the flower you pick is not something rare? The little white slipper, Cypripedium candidum, was last reported in Nodaway County in 1947, but it's no longer found in Missouri. "Collecting pressure and loss of habitat have made this species very rare through the U.S.," according to the book "Missouri Orchids."

It's all right to dig up the flowers if the place they are in will be logged or torn up by developers very soon. But keep in mind that some of them, orchids especially, depend on a fungus in the soil to help break down nutrients so they can be absorbed by the roots. The fungus may not survive the transplant, and that means the flower won't either.

If you want to make a woodland garden, however, there are many sources for native plants -- people don't have to rob forests of their prizes. The Missouri Department of Conservation sells wildflowers propagated and raised in state nurseries.

Area nurseries and greenhouses also sell wild ginger, monarda, Virginia bluebells, wild geranium (not to be confused with the annual geraniums, the Pelargoniums), and Missouri primrose. They also have prairie species such as coneflowers, shooting star, and liatris.

Wildflowers make me think of the word "renaissance," because the word means "new life." I see them and know that Easter's right around the corner, that day of resurrection greeted with thundering hymns. Spring is the best season of them all.

Great Organic Soil Additives to Make Healthy Soil

Every gardener wants to have huge, healthy plants. One of the keys to getting healthy plants is the proper care and feeding of the soil.

I'm not talking about chemical fertilizers. They put nutrients in the plant, sure, but they don't add anything to the soil. When you add plenty of organic material to the soil, you start a process that works for both plants and soil.

When microorganisms break the organic material down, their work and byproducts make the soil looser and more crumbly.

Worms, attracted to the organic matter, further break the nutrients down and then expel it in the form of worm castings. If you've ever dug into the ground to find a worm burrow that's encased in plant roots, you've seen for yourself how much plants love worms. Also, the burrows bring air deep into the ground and ease soil compaction, which is also good for roots.

So keep adding that manure and compost to the ground. (If the manure isn't rotted or composted, you might bury it or cover it with mulch so you don't get an explosion of weeds from it.) But did you know there are other things you could add to perk up the soil?

Grass clippings and mowed-up leaves are great ingredients for the garden. But there are tons of other ingredients you can add to the ground to improve it.

Greensand – This is an undersea deposit that contains many of the nutrients and minerals you'd find in seawater. It's an especially good source of potash. The plants enjoy all the trance minerals found in greensand. Apply this at about a quarter pound per square foot of soil.

Blood or bone meal – Blood meal is a fine source of nitrogen while bone meal provides phosphorus. There has been some concern about these possibly being a source of mad cow disease. Of course, how many cows have acquired the disease in the last year? Five? If you're worried about contracting diseases, then wear gloves when applying it and for heaven's sake don't eat it.

Blood meal is supposed to keep rabbits away. I think that's because all the dogs and cats come into your yard to investigate that delicious smell. Till it in when using, or water it in to avoid visitors.

Fish emulsion – The cats will come running when you start watering your plants with this! But it's an excellent source of nitrogen and the plants love it.

Fish bits – If you've been fishing and have finished filleting your fish, take the stinky parts and bury them in the garden and water them in. Then you'll grow a fish tree! No, actually, fish bits are great for plants. It's said that when the Seneca planted corn, they put a fish in the soil by every plant. It works for roses, too. But water after planting fish so you wash away the fish smell and the animals don't dig it up.

Epsom salts – The magnesium in this stops blossom-end rot in tomatoes and causes roses to grow new canes. Put a half-cup around each plant every month.

Tea and coffee grounds – These contain nitrogen, and make a super mulch for acid-loving plants. They seem to stimulate growth in some plants, too.

Cottonseed meal – Good for adding nitrogen. You might lay this on top of the soil and put a heavier mulch on top to keep it moist and help it break down.

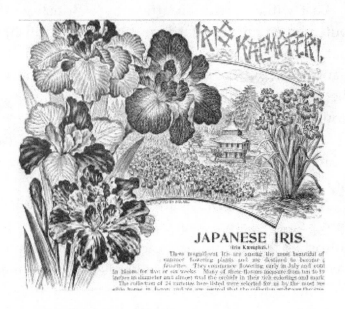

JAPANESE IRIS.

(Iris Kaempferi.)

These magnificent Iris are among the most beautiful of summer flowering plants and are destined to become a favorite. They commence flowering early in July and continue in bloom for five or six weeks. Many of these flowers measure from ten to 12 inches in diameter and almost rival the orchids in their rich colorings and mark. The collection of 24 varieties here listed were selected for us by the most reliable house in Japan, and we are assured that the collection embraces the very

Choose Tough Perennials and Annuals

There's a cute little dayflower growing in the back of my truck, out of the sandbag that I haven't cleared out from last winter.

Actually, the dayflower isn't so cute, since it's wilting from heat and lack of water. But it's hanging in there. When it rains, it revives and gives us cerulean-blue flowers.

Occasionally, social conscience whispers, "What will the neighbors think? Pull it up!" But I can't do it. You've got to respect something that survives despite such oppressive odds. Besides, anything that tough would probably fight its eviction, even bite.

I've seen dayflowers hybridized for larger flowers being sold as annuals under their scientific name, *Commelina*. Would that be a sure bet for a garden that doesn't get much care? You bet.

Last winter I read an article by a British garden writer (but who among the garden writers isn't British) who said that every time she left the garden for a time, the wimpy plants died but the tough plants survived. She said that if she left the garden alone often enough, after a while it wouldn't need her anymore.

That's my garden, filled with plants that can take a licking and keep on, er, growing, come drought, floods, inquisitive dogs, men with lawnmowers, etc.

Native plants always are the best bet. They have put up with Missouri conditions for ages, so whatever the weather unleashes will be old news to them. Heck, any plants that have been run over by buffalo herds time and time again are exceptionally good candidates.

Lately we've been seeing a lot of these prairie plants, such as black-eyed Susan (or *Rudbeckia*), as well as the popular coneflower which is the *Echinacea* of pharmaceutical fame. (This plant has survived buffalo, but who knows if it will survive poachers who dig it from the wild for its roots. This goes double for ginseng.)

Buzz through a copy of *Missouri Wildflowers* (available from the Missouri Department of Conservation) to meet tough plants like joe-pye weed, queen-of-the-prairie, perennial geraniums, spiderwort and pinks. Many of these can be bought through catalogues or local nurseries.

When you plant them, don't coddle them or water the heck out of them. This goes for tulips, too. Did you know that, in their native habitat, they face hot, dry summers? So if you heavily water and fertilize the annuals the tulips grow under, they won't do well next year. Replicate the plant's original habitat, and the plant is happy.

A LOVELY PURE WHITE

The Romance and History of Roses

In the *Iliad*, written 2,700 years ago, Homer writes about Hector's body being rubbed with the oil of roses after his death, and mentions that Achille's shield was decorated with roses. The island of Rhodes (Greek for roses) was known for rose cultivation; they even had coins with roses on them.

Greek mythology was overrun with roses, but the Romans, who stole everything the Greeks did, really went crazy for roses. Horace wrote about how rose cultivation was taking place at the expense of the corn harvest. Martial wrote: "O Nile, the Roman Roses are now much finer than thine! Your roses we need no longer: but send us your corn."

They created hot houses for winter rose bloom. Cleopatra, not to be outdone, filled her banquet hall with roses, nearly knee-deep, when she greeted Marc Anthony.

As a result, the rose became something of a decadent symbol, so when Rome fell, the flower nearly vanished. Roses were grown in monastery gardens for medicinal purposes, which it was highly valued for.

During Islamic expansion, the rose became popular when the Arabs arrived back from north Africa with their seedlings and rose hips. The Moors of Morocco were growing red and white roses in the 9th century, and there was plenty of rose breeding going on. The rose became the holy plant of Islam, and in the middle east, the rose garden became a thing of beauty though it had faded out of sight in Europe at the same time.

In the 1500's, there were few rose species in Europe. The European botanists took only cuttings of the rose – never planted any of the rose hips, because starting roses from seeds was boring. The rose at least came back into favor as a symbol of the Crucifixion and as Mary's flower.

In the 1700's, botanical explorers started bringing home new and interesting plants. At the time, China was closed to Europeans. So, Robert Fortune shaved his head, donned a queue, and traveled as a Chinese to collect plants. China had climbing roses, unknown in Europe.

Then a young woman named Josephine became Napoleon's wife. While Napoleon traveled all over Europe attacking other nations, she had people in his army and entourage send back rose cuttings and plants from their travels. Cargo ships that were seized by Napoleon's army would forward any roses they found on board to Josephine. Josephine even used diplomatic immunity to cover the ship delivering Chinese roses to her.

She purchased Malmaison, her country home, in 1799, and hired a famous botanist to assemble her rose garden. And the nice thing was that if anyone requested a cutting, she'd send it.

From southwest Asia and Afghanistan, the explorers brought the yellow roses to Europe – something that had never existed in Europe before. However, the roses were puny, didn't smell good, and were plagued with blackspot. But once the rose breeders caught on to the knack of crossing the roses so the crosses bore yellow roses (you have to take the seedlings and cross them with the parent yellow to get the right seeds), rose breeding exploded. Victorian England was awash in roses, and new rose families sprang up – Bourbons, Portlands, Hybrid Perpetuals (this includes American Beauty), and of course the Hybrid Teas, which bear blossoms through the entire growing season, not just in spring and fall.

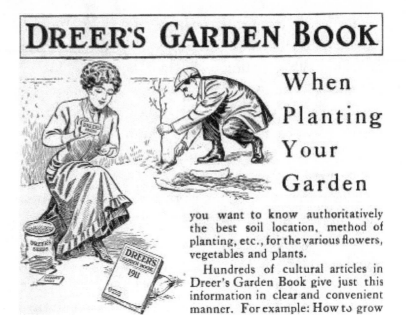

DREER'S GARDEN BOOK

When Planting Your Garden

you want to know authoritatively the best soil location, method of planting, etc., for the various flowers, vegetables and plants.

Hundreds of cultural articles in Dreer's Garden Book give just this information in clear and convenient manner. For example: How to grow

Time to Plant Your Vegetable Garden!!

Here in Missouri on March 25th, according to the University Extension Center, you can plant broccoli plants, Brussel sprouts plants, carrots, collards, kale, head lettuces, mustard, onions, peas (though cowpeas must wait until May), radishes, and turnips. I assume you can also put garlic and shallots into the ground at this time, too.

Swiss chard goes in on April 15.

Though conventional Grandma wisdom states that potatoes can be planted on March 17th, the University Extension Center recommends planting them on April 1st. All I have to say about this raging controversy is that you have to find out what makes *your* potatoes in *your* garden happy. Perhaps you could plant part of your stock now and wait to plant the rest on April Fool's Day, and see what turns out best -- or even if you notice any difference between the two crops. Be sure to note results in your gardening journal for next year's planting.

You Can Plant Trees and Shrubs in March

There's not much nursery stock at the local garden centers yet. However, if you have a hard-to-obtain tree or shrub you wish to make a special order for, this would be a good time to request it. Right now, suppliers have plenty of stock and more time to get it to you. It's going to be a different story in a month or two, when business really booms.

You can plant your trees and shrubs now if you just can't wait. Be sure to take a few precautions to ease them through the remaining cold.

After it's planted, water it, then mulch it well, making a wide, doughnut-shaped area around it, keeping the mulch away from the trunk. Decomposing mulch piled against the trunk will burn the tree -- not surprising, when you consider that the mulch and the tree are made of the same materials.

It is not necessary to wrap the trunk. That is done to keep winter wind from scouring away the tree's moisture, but since winter is close to being over, there's no cause for worry.

If rabbits are a problem in your area, wrap chicken wire around the tree. Keep the wire six inches away from the tree, or the rabbits will press their little pink noses right through and start gnawing.

Once you get the tree planted, you won't see much going on above the ground for about another month. However, below the ground, the tree will have a head start in getting established. When summer's heat and drought arrive, it will be ready.

Lawn Care in Early Early Spring

Take care of your lawn now. Rake away the heavy, wet leaves from last year, but don't rake so vigorously that you take all the new grass with them. Sow grass seed, covering it with straw mulch to protect it from erosion and drying winds. Try not to let the seed dry out. You may have to keep running outside with the sprinkler to keep up with the sun and wind on pleasant days.

In your existing lawn, put down pre-emergent herbicide for summer weeds and crabgrass before the dandelions bloom. Don't put pre-emergent where you've sown grass, because those seeds will not germinate. You will have to wait for the grass to mature before you put down any post-emergent herbicide, too – it will harm the grass when the grass is young and tender.

Late March and Early April are Better Times for Potato Planting

It's warm enough for potatoes now. Cut the potatoes a day or two before planting and keep them in a warm, humid place so the cuts will heal and not be prone to rotting in the ground. Each chunk of potato should have an eye or two. If the potato is egg-sized or smaller, plant it whole. Some people dust the potato with fungicide after cutting, some don't.

Don't plant potatoes next to a gravel road, or in a place that has recently been limed. These alkaline soils encourage a disease called "scab," which creates rough spots on the potato. Keep the wood ashes away from the potatoes, too.

Space the seed potatoes a foot apart in a six-inch-deep trench with a little compost in it. Cover them with four inches of soil. When the vines are four to six inches tall, mound the soil around them higher and higher so tubers can grow, protected from the light. (Light creates green areas on the potato, which are poisonous.)

You might lay the seed potatoes directly on the ground and cover them with mulch as they grow, mounding up the mulch to form hills. Some people plant their potatoes in an old bushel basket filled with mulch. The bottom of the basket should be punched out. To harvest, reach into the mulch and dig around to find the spuds you want. They come out pretty clean when you use this method. Also, using the mulch is good for the garden, when you scatter out the composted mulch at year's end.

PEAR-SHAPED GOURD.

Trellis Planting

I've set up four poles about three feet apart for the vining plants: peas, melons, and pole beans. I'm going to thread twine back and forth between them to give the plants something to climb up. I'm really interested in seeing how the melons turn out when grown this way. They're the "Sakata Sweet," a baseball-sized yellow melon that should take to a trellis with no problem. Cantaloupes, honeydew, and cucumbers can be grown this way, too. This gets the fruit off the ground and up in the air where you can harvest it more easily.

If you have visions of your trellis-grown cantaloupe breaking prematurely off the vine and smashing on the ground, you might start collecting old pantyhose or onion sack webbing so you can make little hammocks for the melons. If you go that route, you might also contemplate giving your cantaloupe a canopy to keep off the sun and a tiny tropical drink, the kind with the paper umbrellas in it. Then, this summer while you're weeding in the sweltering sun, you can rest assured that at least *somebody* is having fun in the garden.

Cold Frames

My cold frame, in which I started vegetables in mid-February, is getting results. Lettuce, carrots, and beets are small but have started growing their true leaves. The lettuce is about an inch and a half tall, and has red speckles all over it (it's a variety called "Red Sails"). I'm hoping that by the time the newly-seeded vegetables start growing, the cold frame vegetables will be ready to harvest.

I am definitely going to plant the cold frame this fall; seeing the results I've gotten with a late winter planting, it would be silly not to.

April

Your Early April To-Do List

* Time to get to work in the vegetable garden! You can plant peas, lettuce, potatoes, beets, broccoli, cabbage, carrots, cauliflower, Chinese cabbage, collards, endive, kale, kohlrabi, mustard, onions, parsley, parsnips, radishes, rhubarb crowns, and turnips.

The window is closing for planting broccoli, Brussels sprouts, carrots, collards, kale, kohlrabi, and head lettuce, so get them in the ground as soon as you can.

Stuff to plant after the 10th of April: parsley, parsnips, rhubarb crowns, and Swiss chard (on the 15th).

For more information on the above planting date, visit your local University Extension center and pick up the Vegetable Planting Calendar. I'm using the MU guide for the above dates, but I'm sure the KU guide has the same information.

* Save the leaves you rake up during spring cleanup. Chop them up with a mower and use them as mulch on your garden once the plants come up. It sounds like we're

heading toward another drought, so you'll definitely need the help come summer.

Speaking of drought, have you noticed that drought is almost a yearly occurrence? I think it's time to stop calling it a drought ... and start calling it "normal weather." The weather's changed, folks, in both summer and winter: when I was a little girl, in the winter we'd get piles of snow, and we'd build snowmen and snow forts and igloos. Now I go out with my little girl and we have to scrape snow from around the yard so we have enough to build a dinky snowman.

Zone 6 is sneaking up on us. The sooner we adjust for this reality, the better. Save water by planting flowers that can take heat and drought, and cut back on watering the grass.

* Topping is that obscene practice of cutting trees to a tall stump, supposedly to keep the tree to a more manageable size. Ha! It's evil, that's what it is, and don't let anyone tell you otherwise.

Why? Consider a tree that's whole and healthy. This tree has a pattern to the way it branches, a pattern that is structurally sound and beautiful. Compare the almost symmetrical pattern of a gingko to the smooth, vaselike structure of an elm, or the chunky shape of a catalpa.

Now consider the tree immediately after it's been topped: a tall stump. Now there's a feast for the eyes.

But you also realize that hey, this tree has no branches, no leaves – therefore, no way to produce food. The tree has to kick into overdrive and grow to survive. This has three immediate results:

1) The tree has to use all of its stored food. If the tree were a human, it would be burning both fat and muscle to survive.

2) These fast-growing branches, like anything else that's built quickly, are shoddy and brittle.

3) The branches are not growing from secure junctures on the tree that are part of the tree's natural architecture, but instead are weakly attached. It won't take as much wind to tear these new branches out. And these straight-line branches will grow back to their original height, or higher.

Once those branches grows back, you have the same problem you had before – a big tree – except now this tree is bigger, weaker, dog-ugly, and it's dropping twice the litter it used to, all because you topped it. Is this what you want?

A better option would be to cut this tree down and then plant a smaller, more manageable tree. When you put the right tree in the right place, then there's no problem.

*Looking for a little manure to use in the garden or compost pile? Call around to your local stables. They are begging folks to take away their manure and they want to share the bounty. They'll even load up your truck for you.

What Plant Tags Actually Mean

The problem with plant tags is that the copywriters are not allowed to tell the unvarnished truth about the plant, even if the plant is a real dog. If they do speak, highly suspicious things happen to them. However, I was able to wrest a few secrets out of one copywriter before she met her doom in a freak rose accident. Here's a primer on what the plant tag says … and what it actually means.

Reseeds freely – And will replace your entire lawn with tiny, wicked clones

Fast-growing vine – Plant it and run

May be invasive – Resistance is futile. You will be assimilated

Easy to care for – Will require care!

Low-maintenance – Will require maintenance!

Fragrant flowers – Even as the rest of the plant defoliates freely due to blackspot/small hungry bugs/evil imps

Size varies – From the size of a breadbox to the size of your house.

Vigorous – To the detriment of every plant around it

Many uses for this plant – None of which you have ever heard of

Semi-dwarf – About a few inches shorter than normal

Disease-free rose – Ha ha ha ha ha!

Fashionable – For the next five minutes, after which it will become an embarrassment

Old-fashioned – With all the ill-mannered traits that made plant breeders scramble to hybridize it.

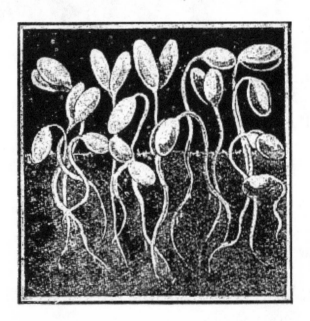

Damping-Off Disease and How to Stop It

I had a bout of damping-off disease in my greenhouse, and it was a mess. Damping-off is a fungal disease that causes newly-planted seedlings to keel over and melt away. It spreads out in a circle, as most funguses do (consider "fairy rings," which are circles of mushrooms on the forest floor), killing off seedlings as it spreads outward.

I haven't had damping-off before, since I keep stuff more on the dry side in the greenhouse, which the fungus doesn't like. However, we had cloudy, cold weather for a whole week, and my trays of seedlings, watered on a Sunday, would not dry out for the rest of the week. No sun, and I couldn't turn on the fans to pull the air through because it was too cold. Humidity was high. All the conditions were right for the fungus to strike.

Then the disease got into the snapdragons I'd just planted and started knocking them out everywhere. I called everyone I could think of for help. Then I took their advice, and it worked.

The best defense is a good offense. Keep a fan running at all times to keep the air circulating. You should feel the air moving through the whole room, but you don't have to turn it up so high that it blows the mice out from under the floor. Keep the plants spaced apart to let air move between them. The fungus likes high humidity and temperatures about 70 degrees. The fan keeps the humidity and temperature lower.

This will break your heart, but get rid of everything that's been infected by the fungus. Dump out the soil and the plants with them, and take the waste outside so spores won't reinfect the plants. As soon as you see the plant keel over, and you know it's not due to being underwatered, out it goes.

If it's a really valuable tray of seedlings, you might dig out the infected plants, isolate the tray from all the other plants, and try a soil drench of Captan fungicide (follow label directions). However, don't bank on saving the seedlings.

A Collection of Sweet-Scented Evening Bloomers.
Sweet Nightingale or Ghost Flower.
Sweet Scented Stocks, Mathiola.
Evening Primrose.
Nicotiana.
Sweet-scented 4-O'clock.
Sweet-scent. Moon Flower.
A large pkt. of all these 6 kinds, mixed in equal portions, over 100 seeds, 5c.

Get a Jump on Weeds

After a good spring rain, everything has greened up beautifully, including the weeds. Get on them. Put the pre-emergent down on the lawn, pull up the weeds in the flowerbeds, and hoe out the vegetable garden. (However, skip tilling if you've tilled the garden in the last year or two. Let the worms have their day. Also, tilling brings dormant weed seeds to the surface where they can sprout.)

By catching the weeds while they're still young and tender, you save yourself a lot of work. Also, a clean garden is a great morale-booster when it's time to plant.

Rabbits, Squirrels, and Other Nuisances

Rabbits and squirrels are cute, but these animals can be nuisances in the garden. There are several ways to deal with them. (These tips can be used for any other critters that are wreaking havoc in your garden.)

If rabbits nibble on your young trees, you may have to wrap trunk guards around the trees. If you use wire, keep it far enough from the trunk so they can't press their noses through and reach the bark.

If the rabbits and squirrels eat the plants in the garden, try repelling them with mothballs, blood meal, or ground limestone. Or try sprinkling cayenne pepper on the plants. (Be careful sprinkling this so you don't start sneezing your lungs out.) These will need to be replaced after a rain, though.

You can put a chicken-wire fence around the garden, but you'll have to bury it a foot into the ground so the rabbits don't dig underneath. The squirrels will still be able to climb over the top.

You might also set up a low-voltage electric fence low to the ground. One strand should work fine. An electric fence can be run off the AC current from your house; others can be run on batteries, which would provide less of a zap.

Don't use red transformers on the fence, though, since hummingbirds are attracted to them. Also, be sure to keep all the grass trimmed around the fence. Grass or weeds touching the wires can short it out.

With an electric fence, it would probably be a good idea to purchase a voltage tester to help fix it when it shorts out, as well as a warning mechanism that will let you know if the fence is on or off so you don't have to test it yourself. "Is this thing working?" ZAP. "Yep, it is!"

If the rabbits squeeze under the fence because their fur insulates them from the shock, then wrap a little piece of aluminum foil on the fence and put peanut butter on it. When the rabbits touch it with their little wet noses, they'll learn to stay away!

Live trapping is also an option. Rent traps from a rental store, bait them with carrots or apples, and then release the rabbits far away.

Gadgets with motion sensors are also available. When a critter ambles by, it will squirt a stream of water to chase it off. Kids love these.

It helps to have a cat or a dog that likes to chase things.

If you live in the country and the rabbits and squirrels are on your property, you can shoot them and serve them for supper, thus keeping down the population.

Shoot animals on your property, though, and nobody else's, because otherwise you would be guilty of trespass and out-of-season hunting. This is also true of any live trapping you may do.

Every one of Them a
. . .Sparkler. . .

has been a favorite in all gardens where good soils
are planted for the past twenty years. There are

A True Blue Rose: Is It Possible? So Far, No.

The other day, I was floored to read in an online message board that some people insisted that blue roses existed and they were actually quite common.

That opens up a can of genetically engineered worms. Those so-called "blue" roses you see in catalogues – and these are the roses that people above are referring to – are actually mauve, lilac, purple, but not true blue. Also, the photos in the catalogue are doctored so the roses look blue. It's just what some folks do when they want to sell plants.

Technically, blue roses – and I mean sky-blue or delphinium-blue roses – **cannot** exist in nature. It's not for lack of trying; breeders have worked for centuries to breed blue roses. It is said that the Arabs, who were very much in love with roses, created a rose that bloomed blue. But it wasn't through breeding. Supposedly they carefully cut the bark of the roses' roots, applied indigo to the cuts, bound the cuts tightly, then replanted the rose. The indigo would have to be reapplied every year to keep the rose blue.

A true-blue rose in nature is impossible because roses lack the delphinidin gene, the one gene that provides the blue pigment the rose needs. So the rose lacks blue genes, sorry about the pun.

"Okay," says the gentle reader, "Then why can't researchers just plug in a gene from a blue plant into the rose's DNA?"

They have. In 1991, researchers cloned delphinidin genes from a petunia. A few years later, they'd figured out how to genetically change roses to accept the gene. Result: a genetically modified rose that had a high level of delphinidin. However, after the addition of the gene, the rose's blooms were a dark burgundy. Not blue.

And this is where it really gets hairy. The blue gene wasn't showing up in the flower because another gene was blocking it. That gene needed to be "switched off" in order for the blue gene to make its appearance.

So in 2001, researchers used new gene technology to switch off the troublesome gene and insert the blue genes. This yielded a rose with high levels of delphinidin in its petals. At last!

But the rose bloomed mauve, not blue. What happened this time?? Well, guess what, the pH level in the rose petals was too acidic for the blue to be properly expressed. The pH of your average rose petal is 4.5, which is moderately acidic.

Remember those bigleaf hydrangeas? You can modify the color of their bracts just by changing the acidity of the soil, right? Give them acid soil and you get pink bracts. Give them alkaline, or sweet, soil, and the bracts turn blue. What do you know, roses are exactly the same way.

So now we have a rose that is genetically capable of being blue. Now researchers are searching for a way to lower the acidity of the rose petals – more genetic tinkering.

One has to wonder, though, what tricks the rose has in store for us. That once we fix one gene, another surprise pops up. The true-blue rose might still be years away.

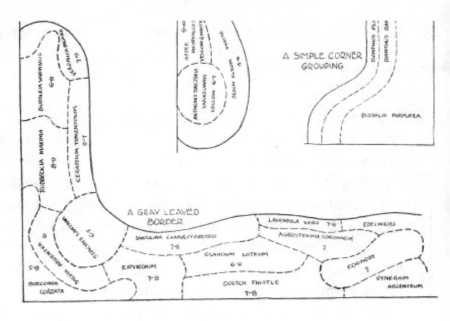

Try Something New in Your Perennial Garden This Year

It's amazing, the number of new and intriguing perennials that swamp the market every spring. It's also hard to wade through all the choices and settle on only a few — there's only so much space in the garden, after all. But lately, these perennials have been doing double duty, adding color through flowers and foliage, which now comes in neat colors or variegations.

The "Black Beauty" elderberry is a gorgeous shrub that has dark burgundy foliage and huge plates of tiny pink flowers in June and July. I'm going to get one of those. Elderberries can be invasive, but birds will love the berries that mature in late August and September. And that dark foliage will fit in well with my color scheme. It's a native shrub, too. I don't have time for wimpy plants. If they can't take what nature throws at them, they can go away somewhere and wilt.

Dicentra "Gold Heart," is an old-fashioned bleeding heart with screaming chartreuse foliage. There seem to be lots of chartreuse plants hitting the market, such as coral bells (Heuchera) "Lime Rickey," an 8-inch-tall chartreuse plant with ruffled leaves and tiny white flowers.

Veronica "Aztec Gold" is another chartreuse cutie. It's a short plant, good as a ground cover or rock-garden plant, which has blue flower stalks in late spring. The foliage is chartreuse in part shade or gold in full sun, so you can play with it.

Tradescantia, or spiderwort, "Sweet Kate" has golden foliage and the big, three-petaled dark-blue flowers in late spring. These are related to dayflowers, which have the blue flowers and are such weeds, so you know the Tradescantia will do just FINE in the garden. Fortunately, it's less invasive.

Sedums, both the tall, fall-blooming varieties as well as the small ground covers, have lots of variegated varieties. "Mutrona" has a subtle hint of pink among the green. "Frosty Morn" has a green leaf edged with white, while "Purple Emperor" has nice, dark, burgundy foliage with dark pink flowers.

Hostas have of course been popular with their variegated colors. "Jane" is a real knockout with butter-yellow leaves edged with green. "Earth Angel" is subtler, a big, green-leafed plant edged with yellow. It gets 30 inches tall and 2 feet wide, so give it room. "Cheatin Heart" is a little gold-leafed hosta that's 8 inches tall, while "Blue Cadet" has tidy blue leaves and is as tough as nails. "Zippity Do Dah" has tidy, slightly wavy leaves with a nice white edge.

"Revolution" is a neat hosta: it was developed from "Patriot" and "Loyalist," so it has a margin of green that looks like it has been painted on a yellow leaf with bold strokes. Inside the yellow are speckles of green. It's a standout.

Lawn Tips for Spring

It's spring and the grass won't stop growing. Here are a few tips to help you deal with your yard.

First, help your lawn by raising the mowing height for bluegrass and fescues to 2 inches. For heaven's sake, don't scalp the lawn. Scalping is when one cuts the grass so low that only nubs are left. If dust is flying into the air as you mow, you're scalping. This is a bad practice because grass that's scalped is severely stressed -- one shouldn't remove more than the top third of the grass while mowing.

And once the forest of grass blades no longer shades the ground, weed seeds are able to germinate. Since weeds grow faster than grass, there will be a nice crop of dandelions the next time you come out to mow.

Cutting the grass too low also curtails its rooting system. A taller grass will have a more extensive root system than grass that has been cut down to little nubs. Shallow roots means a faster drying-out time when the summer heat hits.

Taller grass allows the lawn to shade itself: the roots stay cool, the growth shades out weeds, and less water is needed on the lawn. There's also more leaf surface on the grass, which means more photosynthesis -- greater food production. It means better health overall for the lawn.

That's also why it's a good idea to let the grass clippings fall into the lawn instead of raking them up or bagging them (but do rake them out if the clippings clump on the yard).

University extensions centers are encouraging homeowners to stop bagging grass clippings. Instead, they should let their grass clippings fall back into the grass.

Many think that grass clippings cause thatch. However, that is not the case. Thatch is actually a mat of grass roots and creeping runners -- not clippings. Grass clippings are 75 to 80 percent water. Once the clipped grass withers, which doesn't take long, the remaining bit of grass decomposes quickly. To see for yourself, leave some clippings on your garden border, and watch them for a week or two.

Clippings acts as a light mulch, which keeps grass from drying out, shades out weed seeds and keeps thatch from accumulating in the first place. And keeping the clippings on your yard saves on landfill space – and saves you time.

The benefits don't end there. When you let the clips fall where they may, you can use 20 to 25 percent less fertilizer on your yard. This is because clippings contain 4 percent nitrogen, 1 percent phosphorus and 3 percent potassium, as well as trace minerals.

A layer of clippings also encourages earthworms. They in turn create a healthier soil layer -- their tunneling creates air space in the soil, which the roots need, and earthworm castings are rich food for grass. (You can actually buy earthworm castings, but they are expensive.)

Finally, don't go overboard with the fertilizer. Nitrogen is good on the lawn, but too much of it will make the grass juicy and sweet for insect pests. Also, it makes for lawn-cutting nightmares. Follow label requirements to the letter.

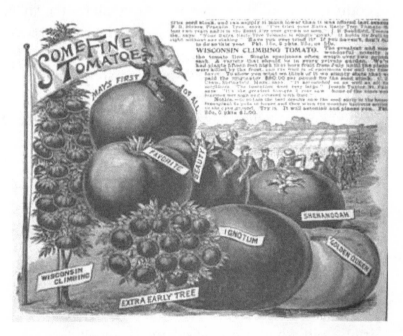

May

A May To-Do List!

May is always a hectic month in the garden, so I'll jump right in.

* Start spraying roses. I never spray insecticides unless I see an actual outbreak of pests, and then I only spot-treat. All insecticides do is damage the population of beneficial insects. However, I will spray fungicides. I prefer to use a systemic fungicide against blackspot and powdery mildew. With a systemic, you can skip a few weeks of spraying and still be okay.

You also need to have your roses mulched for the summer heat. Also, they need a fresh application of compost, and they need to be fertilized monthly. And they need water, lots of water. Do this now so they can get right into blossom mode in June.

* Plant all seeds and plants in your vegetable garden now: It's time! If your plants are already six inches tall, start piling mulch around them to suppress the weeds that will soon compete against them. Use grass clippings, chopped-up leaves and cotton burr compost – anything that will break down into the soil and add humus to keep the worms, and all the tiny critters in the soil, happy. Mulch will also keep the ground cool, and keep that crust from forming on top of the soil that sheds rain like a duck's back.

* If you're tight on space in the vegetable garden, try vertical gardening. Set up poles and twine to grow peas, pole beans, melons, cantelopes, and tomatoes. (The tomatoes you will have to prune to get them to grow this way, but it's worth the effort.) The vines toughen up enough to hold cantelopes aloft, though watermelons might be a different matter.

* In the perennial garden, your late-growing plants should be finally putting in their appearance – hibiscus is one of the slowpokes. Finish cleaning out the leaves and the old sticks, and make a list of what needs to be replaced or divided. Weeds will be a nuisance. Get rid of them fast before they become downright noxious. Dandelions should be dug out, root and all, or they will keep returning. Then mulch, mulch, mulch. Of course!

Annuals can go into the ground, too, if you haven't already put them out.

* When lilacs have finished blooming, prune off the dead blossoms before they start to go to seed, and give the lilac a good dose of compost or other organic fertilizer that will go into the soil. This will help the lilac put its energy into growing itself instead of growing seeds. Also, if you've noticed powdery mildew on the shrubs in the past – an odd white bloom on the leaves – then spray them with a systemic

fungicide, just as you do for roses. Cut down suckers so the lilac doesn't take over your yard, too.

   * Don't cut back the foliage for tulips, daffodils, or other spring-flowering bulbs until it dies. Grandma always braided the daffodil foliage together, and that seemed to get it out of the way.

   * Put some netting over your newly-developing strawberries before the birds figure out what you have there. You might have to suspend the netting over the plants, using small sticks or poles, to keep the birds at a distance. If the netting's directly on top of the plants, a robin might sidle up to the edge of the strawberry bed and start helping herself, though she wouldn't be able to get to the berries in the middle. Or maybe you'd be fine with sharing a few berries: You decide.

The Wonderful New Rose,—
CRIMSON RAMBLER.

Rose Tips for May

May's always rose month for me – the month you have to get those roses going for the big blooms in June, as well as prepare them well for summer's heat and drought, as well as blackspot and aphids and sundry other diseases. A well-prepared rose will bless you with blossoms upon blossoms even through the worst heat.

Start with fertilizer. I like to give the roses everything I have this time of year. Bradfield is a great organic fertilizer, and it contains alfalfa, which really makes the roses sit up and grow. Fish emulsion is great, too, though it will attract the flies as soon as you mix it up, and cats are really interested in it, too. But what's a couple dozen cats compared to great blossoms?

Or give roses the gift of compost. My daughter and I visited the Henry Doorly Zoo in Omaha a week or two ago, and we got a noseful of the compost they'd put on the roses in the Garden of the Senses. (How appropriate.) But you know those roses are going to reward those groundskeepers next month, and there will be no way anyone's going to notice the compost smell then! Compost enriches the soil, and the earthworms love it. The more worms in the garden, the healthier the soil is.

Whatever fertilizer you have, the roses should be fertilized at least twice this month.

The next key to happy roses is water. Not only are roses heavy feeders, but they need lots of water to be happy. Have you turned on your drip lines yet? Do it now if you haven't. We are still in the midst of a drought, and there's no relief in sight. They should be watered every week, the equivalent of an inch of rainfall. Don't think that the roses will get enough water from the rainfall we've been having. After a shower, dig into the mulch to see how far the rain's trickled down. Chances are that it hasn't even gotten past the upper layer, much less to the roots.

This is the time to be spraying for blackspot and powdery mildew, too, or the roses will turn into what my friend Ronna calls "blackspot on a stick." You can use lime sulfur at summer strength, though you can't spray it if the temperature goes over 90 degrees. Though rugosas usually don't tolerate spraying, I've found that they will take a systemic fungicide without any trouble. The systemic fungicide also helps keep the roses clean longer, in case you miss a week or two. But whatever you use, be sure the roses are sprayed every week.

And keep an eye out for rose rosette, which spreads like crazy when the weather is hot and dry. This virus can be fatal disease to roses. Infected roses develop soft, fast-growing shoots, usually a purplish- or bronze-red, that extremely thorny.

Leaves are bumpy or pebbly; sometimes they seem to be more leaf-veins than leaf, as if they've suffered herbicide damage. Blossoms are cabbage-shaped and tiny.

If infected growth is coming directly out of a cane, cut the cane off. Otherwise, the disease will spread through the cane, and eventually through the whole rose. Then watch the rose for any more occurrences of the growth.

However, if the growth comes from the bud union, that means the whole rose is infected. Dig up the rose and burn it. Rose rosette is a virus. There is no cure except for preventive maintenance.

Organic Lawn Care Tips

Here are five easy and organic ways to make your lawn look nice.

First, stop bagging your grass clippings, and let them fall to the ground when you mow. By doing this, you can use 20 to 25 percent less fertilizer on your yard. clippings contain 4 percent nitrogen, 1 percent phosphorus and 3 percent potassium, as well as trace minerals.

Clippings also act as a light mulch between mowings, keeping grass from drying out, shading out weed seeds, and keeping thatch from accumulating. Since grass clippings are 75 to 80 percent water, they wither and get out of sight quickly. Do the same in fall with leaves – shred them and rake them into the grass.

Grass clippings do not cause thatch, but if thatch – a mat of grass roots and creeping runners – already exists in your yard, they can make the thatch problem worse. Rent or borrow a dethatcher to fix the problem.

Use a mulching mower. This kind of mower will cut the clippings into smaller bits than a regular mower would. Fewer clipping, less raking, less work.

Don't let the clippings clump – rake them up and put them on your garden. It makes a nice, soft mulch that unfortunately vanishes after a month or two. So keep adding it. (I pick up extra clippings at the landfill. Just be sure the grasses you're picking up haven't been sprayed with herbicides. I get those with small weeds and clovers among the grass – no herbicides there.)

Second, sow endophytic grasses. Endophytic grasses contain a fungus that lives inside fescue and ryegrass in a symbiotic relationship. The fungus has a nice home, and the grass tastes nasty to diseases, bugs, and animals – the same way that fungus makes moldy bread taste awful. These endophytic grasses are great lawn grasses, since they are resistant to the diseases that regular grasses get. No bugs, no fungus. These are more expensive than regular grasses, of course, and you'll need to plant them as soon as possible to be sure the fungus remains viable inside the grass seeds.

Third, keep the grass high, at least 2 ½ or 3 inches tall, so it shades and mulches itself. Tall grass shades out weeds and keeps the roots cool. When you cut the grass low, then it gets stressed and is more likely to catch diseases.

Also, tall grass is more pleasant to walk and lie down in.

Fourth, maintain your lawn mower. Keep the blade sharp and balanced so grass is cut cleanly, instead of torn. Change the crankcase oil when needed, clean the carburator filter, and check the spark plug. Mowing will go a lot faster and more efficiently. Also, guess what, you'll save gas.

Fifth, mulch the grass by spreading compost, well-rotted manure, Bradfield fertilizer (with the alfalfa in it) or greensand on it. Get the spreader, pile in the goods, then walk up and down and spread the good stuff all over your yard. Feed the soil, and the grass will show you how happy it is.

Then get some local earthworms at the bait shop (or better yet, their eggs) and dig them into the soil all over the lawn. Water all of it in. Let the worms aerate the soil and turn everything under for you. Healthy soil has lots of earthworms, but the ground won't be healthy unless you feed it the organic materials that it needs.

Potato Blight Also Affects Tomatoes

Last year my Celebrity tomatoes developed dark blotches, often when the tomatoes are still very small and green. Each time the blotches quickly spread over the whole fruit and turned it into brown mush. I was aggravated. I had one tomato that I thought had finally made it to maturity, but when I picked it up, I found it had been half-eaten by this rot.

This wasn't limited to the tomatoes touching the ground, either; tomatoes up in the air were also getting these blotches. And, even stranger, my other tomatoes across the garden were doing just fine.

My tomato had late blight, the same disease that caused the great potato famine in Ireland. (Potatoes and tomatoes are in the same plant family, so they share many diseases.) It develops in wet, humid, cool conditions – the kind of weather that my tomato plants had been experiencing.

When you have a blighted tomato, one side of the fruit may look lovely, but the other side turns a brownish-black with the disease.

The leaves on plants affected by blight have little brown spots on them, as if a few drops of acid fell on them. On the back of the leaves, or on their tops, is a lot of white, powdery mold.

It should be noted that there's been a worldwide resurgence of the disease in both potatoes and tomatoes. In some places, the fungus has developed resistance to systemic fungicides. However, external fungicides – those that resist fungus by changing the pH of the outside of the plant – still seem to do the trick *if you start spraying them after you plant your tomatoes and potatoes*. Keep on the fungicide, especially if there's a rainy time forecast. Copper spray, also known as Bordeaux, also seems to help as a preventative measure.

The drawback is that the fungicide will have to be reapplied every time it rains. Also, by the time blight has appeared on your tomatoes, it will be too late for a fungicide to do any good. It can be used only as a preventative measure.

However, some experts are not sure how much good spraying actually does, so you might take notes about your spraying program and see what works and what doesn't.

One way of outsmarting the disease may be to plant a wide variety of disease-resistant tomato plants, not just one variety. Even if you lose one or two tomato plant to the disease, perhaps the other varieties will resist it. Also, space the tomato plants well apart from each other. Due to my poor planning (which, in hindsight, turned out to be good planning), my tomato plants were scattered around the garden. This turned out very well for me.

Mulch the potatoes and tomatoes very well to avoid water splash-up from the soil. Sometimes spores are spread onto the plant this way. Also, water early in the day so the plant has time to dry off before nightfall. Don't plant tomatoes where you had any potatoes, tomatoes, eggplants, or peppers the previous year.

Give potato and tomato plants plenty of space in the garden for good air circulation. You might trim off parts of your tomato plant, especially if it's a monster plant, to let the air travel through.

As soon as you see infected fruits or foliage, remove them and burn them. (Don't compost them unless your pile stays really, really hot.) Bag them up and get them out of the garden so no more fungus spores can spread. (Spores come out of the fruiting bodies in the brown spots.)

Some tomato plants, such as Mountain Fresh, Mountain Supreme, and Plum Dandy, show resistance to the disease.

When you fertilize, keep the nitrogen levels low. Nitrogen makes leaves juicier and more succulent for diseases.

Don't save seeds from infected crops, since the disease can be spread through the seeds.

If blight gets out of control, you'll have to pull up and destroy a lot of plants. So, get rid of any infected material as soon as you see it and keep spraying the fungicide.

May's Favorite Pickling

Some Quick Reminders for Late May

* Watch for pine sawflies on Mugo and Scotch pines. You can see them when you wave your hand over the shrub. The caterpillars respond by waving their upper bodies around. A few applications of insecticidal soap will fix them.

* Watch out for striped and spotted cucumber beetles (aka green ladybugs). They can spread wilt and mosaic virus to squash and cucumber plants, ruining your harvest.

* Scale crawlers are active right now. (Scale, an oyster-shell-shaped pest found on roses and fig trees, can actually move around in its juvenile stage.) Spray dormant or horticultural oil to smother them.

* Don't cut back tulip, daffodil, or hyacinth foliage while it's green. The leaves are producing starches to be stored away in the bulb for next year. Wait until it browns to cut it off. My grandma braids hers to get them out of the way.

* Slugs love the rain. Sprinkle diatomaceous earth around plants, especially hostas. The diatomaceous earth (which looks like pulverized chalk) should be replaced after every rain. Also, chalk drawings on the sidewalk can also kill slugs. (I've seen it, and believe me, it's not pretty.)

I've heard that you can set out saucers of beer, and the slugs will crawl into them and drown. Unfortunately, raccoons like this too, and it is a bad thing to have drunken raccoons staggering and yowling outside your house at 3 a.m. (Note: this has never happened to me.)

Fragrance Can Give Your Garden an Extra Dimension

There's always so much emphasis on color, form and texture in the garden. When you think about it, however, a garden really should have more than meets the eye. It really adds a special touch when there's also a strong emphasis on scent in the garden.

That's why herbs are such an asset to the landscape, whether in the vegetable garden, in a formal knot garden, or in the anything-goes-yet-it-looks-so-beautiful English garden. They add color, scent, and even functionality if you need a little thyme and sage for the roast.

Whether you grow herbs for medicinal purposes, for color and show, or to eat, they can really liven up a garden. I love rosemary and lavender; my daughter enjoys collecting leaves off the sage plant. Parsley bores me, but basil is dandy when cooked with yellow summer squash. I grow spearmint in a pot for tea. The pot keeps it from overrunning the world (for the moment).

Many herbs are grown for their foliage. Some, such as tricolor sage, have variegated or colored leaves. Lamb's ear, considered an herb, has soft, silvery leaves. In fact, some gardeners cut off the blossom stalks of lamb's ear, because when the plant is allowed to blossom, the leaves start looking sad and bedraggled. The blossoms aren't very showy, but the leaves really put on a show.

Santolina, also called lavender cotton, is a silver-leaved herb that is used in knot gardens in the same way boxwood is –a tidy shrub that's kept trimmed to edge the garden.

In hummingbird gardens, try pineapple sage. This plant has a sweet pineapple smell; I roam everywhere in order to purchase one of these, just so I can pluck the leaves at my leisure. Though it's an annual, this sweet-scented herb can grow into a small shrub, up to four feet in good soil, and bears brilliant red flowers that hummingbirds love.

And herbs come in so many fragrances. Thyme, verbena, and geraniums can smell like lemon, while mints and basil can smell like chocolate. That's another neat thing about herbs – their versatility.

Herbs can add color and scent to the vegetable garden as well. In this setting, you can harvest entire branches without messing up the overall appeal of your garden.

When harvesting herbs, bear a few things in mind. Gather the leaves or stems before the herbs flower, and keep flowers trimmed off for the best flavor in the leaves. Also, the best time to pick is early in the morning.

Some herbs are invasive. Beware of oregano, which reseeds like mad, and of mints, which send out subterranian runners for miles and can spread faster than you can run. Plant them in containers so they will be contained.

Fresh herbs can be kept for about a week in the refrigerator in a plastic bag with holes punched in it. For longer storage, dry herbs in the microwave. Place four or five stems on a double thickness of paper towels; cover them with a single paper towel. Then microwave them on high for about two to three minutes, until the leaves are brittle. You might also press herbs in odor-free paper to dry them.

Herbs can be frozen, too. Lay them out on a tray and put that in the freezer until they're solid. Then package them up, label them (ALWAYS label them!), and get them back in the freezer.

June

Spotted Cucumber Beetles

Green ladybugs are evil!

Okay, maybe they're not evil, but they sure aren't doing you any favors.

These bugs are actually the spotted cucumber beetle, which eat the leaves of your cucumber plants and other cucurbits (like squash and pumpkins). They can carry bacterial wilt from plant to plant while feeding, and this disease basically causes your plant to wilt and shrivel and die. To make matters worse, its larvae is the southern corn rootworm, and you really want to have those eating the roots of your corn!

These ladybugs eat other plants. I usually find these beetles eating the stamens and petals of white or yellow roses. Then all the petals fall off prematurely.

The adults generally emerge from the ground in early to mid-August. Keep an eye out for them.

I just grab the beetle in my fingers and squish it, but if you don't want bug guts on your fingers, carry a spray bottle of insecticidal soap and spray the beetles when you see them. You might put fine nets over the cucurbits (though watermelon is generally not affected) to keep the beetles off.

Striped cucumber beetles, which may have shown up earlier this season, are also bad for your cucurbits.

To keep numbers down next spring, till up your corn in the fall. This may help expose beetle larvae and kill them. Clean up the garden and burn all cucurbit debris.

Squash Bug Control

Squash bugs are a real problem on squash, watermelon, and cucumber vines. Their reddish or bronze egg masses can be found on the underside of the leaves, and darken when they're about to hatch. The adult bugs are grey and their backs look like a shield. They are often misidentified as stink bugs.

A large number of squash bugs feeding on the plants can cause the vines to wilt badly, but the wilt ends when the overpopulation ends.

To catch squash bugs, lift leaves and crush the copper-colored egg clusters underneath. Clean up plant debris so the bugs have no hiding place. Lay several boards around the plants. Every morning, lift the boards and kill any bugs hiding underneath.

If the bugs are getting out of control, spray insecticidal soap or pyrethrins, but this works best only when the bugs are still small. If you use chemicals like Sevin or Eight, carefully follow label directions, and remember that you won't be able to use those chemicals near the date of harvest. Also, these chemicals can kill off honeybees that are trying to pollinate the flowers. No honeybees, no fruits.

I like using a spray of pyrethrin to kill the squash bugs. Sometimes I carry a bottle with me so I can zap those green ladybugs in the rose blossoms, or the tobacco hornworms on the Nicotine plants.

At the end of the season, destroy all vines and clean up the garden so adults have no place to spend the winter.

Next year, cover vines with a fine-mesh cloth to keep bugs out. Once flowering begins, remove the cloth so bees can pollinate the flowers. By then it will be too late for bugs to do their damage.

ANTIRRHINUM TOM·THUMB

Revamping Your Perennial Bed

It rains. Then it's clear for a few days, and you wait and wait to do a little garden work. When the ground is just dry enough, you head out there with your shovel, whistling the theme from "A Fistful of Dollars" (We can fight!).

Just as you set the shovel in, even as you brace your foot on the shovel to break the ground, the sky breaks open and dumps 55 gallons of water over your head and on your garden, making it impossible to dig. "Tee hee," say the clouds, then they drift away to play the same joke on someone else.

That about describes the last several weeks. Still, I was able to get out recently and get all the perennials moved around in my garden (the 20-foot one). I walked like the Hunchback of Notre Dame for a week after, but I'm glad to be finished with that.

I'd meant to get the perennials all moved around last year, but for some reason or another, I never did it. So, the moving was a little like cleaning out Fibber McGee's closet: Don't open that door!

At one point I had at least 10 plants out of the ground, languishing in the shade of the old lilac (which needs to be rejuvenated badly) as I tried to get enough ground clear and raked level so I could put them back in.

What was neat was that I found several plants that I had believed dead. Two lilies that didn't come up last year were peeking through the soil under some asters, and the same asters were hiding a sedum a friend had given me. And, in a shovelful of soil I was carting out of the way, I found a little delphinium that I thought had succumbed to bacterial spot last summer.

The whole operation went pretty well, and the impromptu design does have some coherence. It looks pretty good until you get to the far right of the garden, the last bit of garden I did.

One of the big rules in garden design is: Buy either three or five of one plant, so you have a drift of color that can be seen.

I disregarded the rule a few times, buying plants that I meant to try them out and then get some more (and never did). So most of the garden's design looks pretty coherent, because I have huge drifts of yarrow and asters (very huge) and Russian sage. But suddenly at the far right of the garden, there's one Shasta daisy, one gallardia, one daylily, etc. It's a mess!

But there's an island bed I need to finish, after I reseed the lawn ...

Deadheading Your Plants

Deadheading has nothing to do with attending Grateful Dead concerts. I'm talking about taking the old flowers off the plant before they set seed, so the plant is encouraged to produce new flowers.

See, the whole meaning of life to a plant (as far as we know, that is) is to produce seed so a new generation of plants will grow after the mother plant dies. When you remove the flower as it loses color, the plant turns all its energy toward producing more flowers instead.

Deadheading keeps the plant looking good, and it allows the plant to save some energy during the endlessly hot summer months.

It's a good idea to rummage through your garden once a week to keep your plants looking fresh and lovely. With roses, you have to catch them after every rain.

Of course, deadheading a rose will be different than tidying up the petunias, and you'll deal with a Shasta daisy differently than you would with the daffodils. Usually, if you have a flower cluster, you can cut back to the next flower. If not, just cut back to the next leaf on the plant.

There shouldn't be much daffodil foliage left right now, but if it's really starting to bug you, cut any dying flower stems back to the ground, then make coarse braids out of the daffodil leaves. The daffodil will still be able to drink in the sun's energy to store for next year, and the braids look a lot tidier than sprawling leaves.

Some plants, like Artemisia "Silver Mound" or catmint, might sprawl after they bloom. Go ahead and cut these plants back severely -- even by 50 percent -- and feed them after you cut them back. The catmint might even give you a second flush of flowers.

Rose bushes are a different breed altogether. When a blossom is fading, cut the stem back to the first leaf that has five leaflets on it. If this is *way* down the stem, then you can settle for a three-leafleted leaf. Then cut the stem, angling the cut away from the bud below the leaf. Don't cut too high, for the leftover bit of stem may become infected. When you cut down to the leaf with five leaflets, you give the rose a good bud to start growing on, and blooming on, later.

Deadheading won't give you instant blooms, of course. Give them a little time. Some will reward you with continuing blooms, while some will wait until fall to reward you. Gardening's not all instant gratification, anyway.

July

July To-Do List

* Now that your strawberry patch has stopped producing, mow it with the mower at its highest setting. Mowing the patch will kill off the old plants and make way for the new ones. Weed the patch, put down some compost and fertilizer, and give it a light mulch of straw. Water the strawberries well to help the plants through the summer heat.

Also, clean up all the strawberry runners that are spreading into different parts of your garden. However, if your patch is getting old, go ahead and manage that spread. Guide them into a new place with fresh soil, then destroy the old patch. They'll readily repopulate an area with new plants if you let them, which may cut down on disease as well as give you more vigorous plants.

I haven't mowed my strawberry patch yet because a little wren that lives in my yard hops under the leaves to find insects. I'd hate to take away her hiding place!

* Raise the mowing height on your lawnmower. The taller grass will shade its roots, keeping them cooler. This also shades out weed seeds so they can't germinate. Taller grass also requires less water. This will help your lawn look decent when the real heat hits and the other lawns start turning brown.

* Keep spraying roses with fungicide every week, keep feeding them every week (even if it doesn't seem like it's doing any good), and keep giving them lots of water every week. But especially keep spraying. This time of year is crucial in the fight against blackspot. To miss a few sprayings means you get blackspot on a stick. Pick off infected leaves and destroy them.

A systemic fungicide might help, too, because with a systemic, you could miss a spraying and be all right. (Systemics are absorbed into the plant, while other fungicides sit on the surface of the leaf and get washed off with water.)

A little compost, rotted manure, or worm castings around the roots of your roses will help repel diseases and insects though good nutrition (which includes feeding the creatures that live in the soil around the rose's roots – feed the soil and you get a stronger plant).

* Keep deadheading flowers. Petunias should be pinched back before they start getting too leggy. Cut mums back after they finish blooming so they'll be ready to bloom this fall.

* Vine borers are a problem on squash vines. These are caterpillars that drill into the vine several inches above the ground, killing the plant when it blossoms. If you notice a sawdust-like substance on the stem, cut into the injured place and dig out the borer. Then pile up soil above the wound. If you've caught the borer in time, the squash will send out new roots and survive.

Another insect to look out for is the large, dark-brown squash bug. Lay boards next to your plants. Every morning, turn the boards over and smash the squash bugs you find there. You can also find and smash the rafts of copper or yellow-colored egg clusters on leaves.

* Leave those suckers growing on your corn plants, and don't remove them. Leaving the suckers to grow on a corn plant actually gives you larger ears of corn than when you remove them.

* My potatoes are setting seeds – actually, sprouting green acorns on strings is more like it. Pick the seeds off so the potato can direct all its energy to its growing tubers. (You can dig out a few tubers now to cook as new potatoes.)

* Epsom salts, which are a good source of magnesium, are great in the garden. Add ½ cup of Epsom salts to the soil around the rosebush twice a year – at the beginning of the season and midway through the season. This encourages basal breaks – buds that become strong, new canes.

You can also add Epsom salts to the soil around your tomato and pepper plants, ½ cup per plant. Doing this will guard against blossom-end rot, those ugly, sunken black spots at the blossom ends of the fruits.

* My grandma and I froze some sweet corn last week. She uses a simple recipe to freeze her corn. You cut the kernels off the cob until you fill up a kettle. Then you scoop out eight cups of corn into another kettle (or any container that will hold it). To the eight cups of corn you add 1 ½ teaspoon of salt, ½ cup sugar, and 1 cup water. Then you mix it together and put it in your little containers, label them, and put them in the deep freeze. No cooking necessary!

When you take out a packet later, defrost it, then cook the corn until it's tender, and it's just as sweet as when you cut it off the cob.

Beat Heatstroke and Heat Exhaustion

Here are some tips on taking the heat when working in the garden or the yard.

First, work in the morning and evening when it's cooler. Keep in mind that soon the early morning temperatures will be hovering in the 80's. Still, it's better to work in 80 degree heat than when it's 95 and the sun on your back feels like a furnace at the metal refinery.

Keep your chances for skin cancer as low as possible. Protect yourself from the sun by wearing a sunblock with a high SPF (sun protection factor). There are some available with an SPF of 45 and 50. Also, wear a wide-brimmed straw hat. The sun is basically one gigantic nuclear explosion; you can't expect to keep all that radioactive stuff off your skin with a little dab of cream. The hat helps to keep you cool, too.

Try to stay out of the sun between 10 a.m. and 2 p.m., if possible, when the sun is at its strongest.

Drink water, or any kind of liquids, often – a few ounces every 20 minutes is good. Cool liquids are readily absorbed by the body.

Heat exhaustion, according to the *American Medical Association Family Medical Guide,* is when the body can't get rid of its excessive heat because it has lost a lot of water and salt through sweating. Symptoms include dizziness and nausea; the person may feel faint. Headache and muscle cramps develop, while the pulse and breathing quicken. If you have these symptoms, get to a cool place and lie down. Loosen any tight clothing, and drink water with a little salt added. (Add a level teaspoonful of salt to a quart of water.) A cool shower would help.

Don't let the symptoms progress beyond this stage, because that will lead to heatstroke, a medical emergency. At this point, the person becomes confused or faints, and has hot, dry skin and a rapid pulse. *Call 911 immediately!*

Take it easy out there. When in doubt, for goodness' sake get in the shade and sit down.

Take Care of Hummingbird Feeders

Hummingbird feeders are out now. Take care of yours.

The Missouri Department of Conservation suggests purchasing a feeder with bee and wasp guards. Coat the string the feeder hangs from with petroleum jelly to keep ants out.

To make nectar, combine one part sugar with four parts water. You don't have to add red food coloring to attract hummingbirds.

It is important to change the nectar weekly, or any time the mixture in the feeder grows cloudy. It is even more important to wash the feeder every week in hot, soapy water. Molds love sugar; they will grow like crazy on it.

If you prefer to plant a hummingbird garden, you have a variety of plants to choose from. Hummingbirds enjoy flowers such as columbines, Monarda (also known as bergamot or bee balm), cardinal vines, geraniums, honeysuckle, and snapdragons. Hummingbirds are attracted to red or orange tubular flowers, but they don't drink from them exclusively. I saw a ruby-throated hummingbird visiting my flax plants, which have sky-blue blossoms.

Hummingbirds also eat small insects and spiders that they may find in the blossoms.

Food Pantry Plea

Does it look like you'll have tomatoes and zucchini coming out of your ears when harvest time rolls around? Share your bounty with the local food pantry. Why waste it when someone can taste it? If you're not sure where your local food kitchen is, ask a pastor or priest. Many churches also hold food drives that you can participate in.

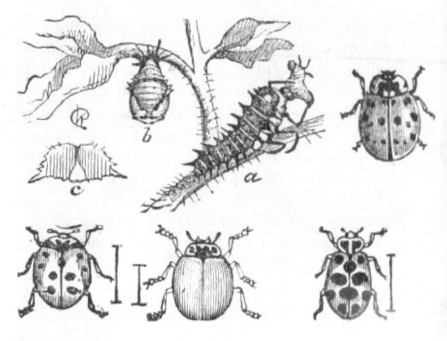

Helpful Tips for Your Lawn

Hot weather, kids out playing, and guys who scalp the lawn with Weed-Eaters can really do a number on lawns. Help your yard through the rest of the summer with these tips.

First of all, mowing. Disconnect the spark plug from your mower, then turn the mower over to look at the blades. One of the biggest causes of grass problems is dull blades, which tear the grass rather than cut it, leaving frayed edges that take longer to heal than smooth cuts.

Sharpen blades once a month, or after eight hours of mowing, for optimal performance. Take the blades to a professional sharpener. If you want to sharpen them yourself, keep that spark plug disconnected, remove the blade and set it in a vise, then sharpen to the original cutting angle. File equal amounts from both ends to keep the blades balanced.

Raise the mowing height for bluegrass and fescues to 3 inches. Grass that's tall and thick will keep moisture from escaping and will allow the roots to stay cool. That's also why it's a good idea to let the grass clippings fall into the lawn instead of raking them up (but do rake them up if they clump on the yard). The clippings act as mulch, releasing nutrients back into the soil.

Scalping is when one cuts the grass so low that only nubs are left. Once the grass blades no longer shades the ground, weed seeds are able to germinate. Also, a tall blade of grass will have a more extensive root system than one that has been cut down to a nub. Shallow roots means a faster drying-out time when the heat hits.

Reduce the amount of nitrogen you feed the grass, or even stop giving your yard nitrogen altogether. Nitrogen makes a grass succulent and soft, and what you want is a lean, mean grass to get through this hot weather. If you fertilize, increase the amount of potassium you give it instead.

Instead of sprinkling chemicals on the grass, feed the grass compost instead. Once a month, scatter a layer of compost over the grass with a spreader or by hand. Compost is super plant food that discourages thatch and adds beneficial micronutrients to the soil, and it suppresses fungal diseases. Worms like it, too. Happy worms equal a healthy soil. (Also, if you get enough activity with worms and other good critters in the soil, they'll help aerate the soil all through the growing season.)

Instead of "feeding" the lawn with chemicals that do nothing to improve the soil, use organic lawn food instead. Spraying the lawn with seaweed extract helps the grass fight heat stress. Fish emulsion and bone meal is also good. Corn gluten meal will keep weed seeds from germinating and adds nitrogen to the soil.

Watering is another way to help the yard. One inch of moisture every week, if it doesn't rain, will give the grass all the water it needs. Water a little extra near buildings and other heat-reflecting surfaces.

Take care not to over-water, especially if the yard is poorly drained or if the soil consists of heavy clay. Over-watering can lead to drowned roots and outbreaks of fungal diseases. Give the grass an inch of water every week. Water early in the morning twice a week for best results. To water during the day or evening invites disease.

(2) SET TREE IN HOLE TRIFLE LOWER THAN IT STOOD IN NURSERY

(3) FILL GOOD)P SOIL UP AROUND \LL. PACK FIRMLY ITH FEET OR SET .E BY FILLING HOLE

GOOD SOIL

(4) LOOSEN BURLAP AT TOP OF BALL AND ROLL BACK OR CUT OFF

August

Prepare Your Garden for a Fall Harvest

If you can put up with the heat, you can start your fall crop of vegetables right now. By doing this, you can get a second harvest before (or even after) frost. Imagine fresh vegetables for Thanksgiving ... or even for Christmas, if you put out the right vegetables and mulch them well.

Fall-grown vegetables taste better due to ripening in the cooler weather, and you have a lot less hassle with insects and diseases.

There's a short window for sowing and planting in this area. Sow beans, beets, carrots, kohlrabi, peas, zucchini, and lettuce (leaf and butterhead), from now until about August 15th. Those dates also go for planting cole crops, if you can find them. Sow mustard, radishes, spinach, and turnips from now to the 30th.

Be sure to buy "short-season" plants to be certain you can get them harvested before frost. (Don't forget, though, that you can extend the growing season with a few old blankets!)

Prepare your garden by taking out any old plants and weeds. Throw out diseased plants and fruits, to avoid re-introducing pathogens into the garden.

Spread compost or aged manure over the ground. You might till it in, but shallowly. Deep tilling will cause the soil to dry excessively. Add a pound of 13-13-13 all-purpose fertilizer per 100 square feet of ground before you cultivate the soil.

The night before you cultivate, water the ground, then water it again a day or two before you plant. Otherwise, you will have to take a chisel to the soil. Once you're done cultivating, get some worms at the local bait shop and add them to the ground to keep the soil happy.

Sow seeds twice as deep as you do for spring planting to keep the seed from drying out during germination. Once the seeds are planted, water daily.

To keep the seeds cool, shade them by placing a board over your rows, raising it off the ground with two flowerpots or bricks. When the seedlings emerge, remove the board, then mulch the ground with a half-inch of grass clippings or straw. Pile on the mulch once the seedlings are 1 to 2 inches tall.

Sometimes it can be hard to get the crops established. Water them well, and use nylon net to protect the seedlings from insects and the hot sun. At least harvesting plants in fall will be a relief, compared to harvesting in the heat of the summer sun.

Mulch makes all the difference once the plants come up, especially since we're going through yet another drought right now. Three or four inches is a good start. Wood chips, grass clippings, shredded leaves, hay or straw, are all good mulches.

If you have a large area of weeds in your garden, stomp them down so they lie flat. Then put over the top of a layer of ten pages of newspapers. (I've found that five pages isn't enough – the pillbugs or rolly-polly bugs will eat through them quickly and allow weeds to push through.) Over the top of the newspapers place several inches of straw or hay or other mulch. It looks great and saves an awful lot of labor. I installed this kind of mulch over my weeds several months ago, and I haven't had any problems with weeds since in those places. (In unmulched areas of my garden, though, it's another story.)

August Lawn Tips

From August 15 to September 15 is the best time to fix up your lawn. Grass seed sown now will have the best chance of maturing before winter and surviving the cold. This is also a great time to renovate the lawn if it needs it, through fertilizing, getting rid of unwanted plants in the lawn, and even aerating or dethatching.

University Extension professionals recommend letting clippings fall back into the lawn – this alone can contribute up to 25 percent of your fertilization needs. The grass clippings, which are mainly made up of water, quickly dry up and break down. Their remains serve as mulch, shading the roots of the grass from the hot sun.

Grass clippings do not lead to a buildup of thatch in the lawn. Thatch is actually a mixture of roots, dead crowns and rhizomes that are resistant to decay. Adding clippings actually cuts down on thatch. (However, if you already have a thatch problem, rent a dethatcher and run it over your yard.)

When you mow, don't remove more than 30 percent of the grass blade, because removing more will stress the grass. On the same note, don't use your weed-eater to scalp the ground. Weeds will take over the bare areas and duke it out with your grass.

The grass height, after mowing, should be 2 1/2 to 3 inches high. Taller grass allows the lawn to shade itself: the roots stay cool, the growth shades out any weeds that are trying to grow, and less water is needed on the lawn. There's also more leaf surface on the grass, which means more photosynthesis -- greater food production. It means better health overall for the grass, and the lawn.

Speaking of food production, too much emphasis is being placed on fertilizing through the spring and summer months. Some fertilizer is needed at this time. However, overapplication (especially of nitrogen) is definitely a problem, causing overly green and juicy grass that insects can really sink their mandibles into. Overly fertilized grass also causes too much growth, resulting in lawn-cutting nightmares.

The best time to fertilize is in August and September, and in late fall, from October through December. This fertilization practice creates a hardier and tougher grass with a deeper root system and slower growth.

Finally, water lawns once a week with an inch of water. A sprinkler set in one spot will give the lawn that inch within the space of one or two hours. Water in the morning, so the water on the grass will evaporate before nightfall.

Fusarium Wilt, Bacterial Wilt, and Other Wilts

Olin Cooper of Pickering, Mo., wrote, "I wonder what invaded my watermelons and muskmelons in the garden last year. Just as the melons started to ripen, the plants died and I did not get a melon from the entire patch. I realized that the same thing may happen this year, since the patch is very close to the same location as last year."

Melons – not only canteloupe, but watermelons – should be planted in different places every year to avoid soil-borne diseases that can survive from year to year. Also, some pests, such as root-knot nematodes, can infest the roots from year to year. Nematodes, or eelworms, are tiny white wormlike creatures that feed on roots. I've noticed that they'll also attack marigolds that are planted in the same spot year after year. In fall, when you pull the marigolds up, the roots are covered with small, knotty galls. The roots of the melons will look the same way.

One bad disease is bacterial wilt. The vines wilt as if they are severely dry, and then they simply croak. Once the vines wilt, there's no chemical that'll bring them back.

When you put out next year's crop, keep an eye out for cucumber beetles. Some of them are those green ladybugs I like to crush because they eat rose blossoms. Other cucumber beetles are green with black stripes. These beetles spread the bacterial wilt disease from plant to plant. Zap these with insecticidal soap every time you get a chance. You really have to move fast, because the beetles will immediately fly away or fall off the plant. Oh, I do not like them one bit!

Another disease is Fusarium wilt. This is a form of the fungus that will also attack tomato plants. Fusarium will start in the roots and move from there into the stems. If your plant is hardly growing and is all stunted, that's probably what the problem is. Then they wilt and die. Sometimes a white fungus starts growing on the dead vines.

If this happens, get the dead vines out of the garden ASAP so the spores don't spread back into the garden. Don't plant any melons or tomatoes there next year, or the next, because Fusarium will stay in the soil for many years. Your best bet is to plant resistant varieties. Next year when you buy tomatoes or melons at the nursery, look on the tag under the plant's name. Often there will be some letters – V, F, L, N – there. These denote what diseases the plants are resistant to.

Just for reference, here is a listing from the Helpful Gardener website:

A - Alternaria leaf spot

F - Fusarium wilt

FF - Race 1 & Race 2 Fusarium (lots of strains out there)

L - Septoria leaf spot

N - Nematodes

T - Tobacco mosaic virus

V - Verticillium wilt

Mainly it's the preventative measures that save us: crop rotation from year to year, quick cleanup of diseased plants, and the merciless slaughter of those blasted cucumber beetles.

Well, Olin, I guess I've written a really depressing gardening column this week! If it's any consolation, all my squash plants have already succumbed to Fusarium wilt. So I have these big, tidy, mulched areas with nothing in them, though the Mr. Stripey tomatoes are already moving into the territory. We'll let them.

Fighting Weeds in High Summer

Keep on top of those weeds. You absolutely must get them while they're small, or even when they're medium-sized. It's not going to be long before they get huge, and when they hit that size, it's easy to just let the garden go.

It's easiest to weed when the garden doesn't look like it needs weeding. Go in there often, even daily, and look under plants, and clean up everything you can. That way, if you do fall behind, you won't have to fight so hard to clean it up.

We're three inches behind on this year's rainfall (not counting last year's deficit,), yet the weeds keep popping up. It got so bad that I rewrote the lyrics to "Turn Around:" "Turn around and they're tiny, turn around and they're grown, turn around and they're six feet tall with seedlings of their own."

If you have a lot of pavement with cracks in it, or stones with weeds among them, there's a neat way of taking care of them. There's a flamethrower (!! Yes, you heard me right) made specifically for weeds. You'll need a small tank of propane to fuel it and a dolly to carry it around. If you don't mind that, then pick up the wand, turn on the propane, light the torch, and burn down the weeds.

I can see the guys reading this column beating down the doors at the local hardware stores to pick up one of these babies.

For those of us who do not want to use a torch and propane tank in 95-degree weather, here are some other ways to deal with weeds.

Get weeds while they're small. It's easiest to weed when the garden doesn't look like it needs weeding. Go in there often, even daily, and look under plants. That way, even if you do fall behind, you won't have to work so hard to clean it up.

Mulch works wonders. A two- to three-inch layer of mulch will keep seeds from germinating. Earthworms like mulch, too; they will tunnel under it, enriching the soil with their castings, keeping the soil aerated and much looser. This will make weeds come out much more easily.

Mulch is free. If you have grass clippings or leaves from last year, carpet your gardens with them. Mulch keeps the soil cool, keeps the ground from drying out, keeps the dirt from splashing all over the plants when you water, makes the garden look tidy, and fertilizes the soil. Mulch is one of the best things you can get for a garden.

Finally, dig out the roots of perennial weeds such as dandelion and plantain. It takes a little time, but it's better to dig the root out once than keep pulling off the leaves every time it grows back out.

Now the tough part.

Q: The weeds have taken over my vegetable or flower garden. What do I do?

A: Go in with the flamethrower and do a little Rambo imitation. Then call the fire department.

Something tells me that firefighters don't get paid enough to put up with stuff like that.

The most important thing to do is to make a dent in the garden. If you have a vegetable garden, then clear the rows with a weed-eater. If you have a flower garden, then grit your teeth and start pulling or hoeing like crazy, even if it means losing a couple of plants.

Give yourself fifteen minutes to do the job. No more than that. If you feel like working longer, then do so.

Then go after the big weeds only. Don't bother with tiny weeds. You have to make a hole in the mess. Once you've made visible progress, your morale goes up, and you feel more capable of tackling the whole thing.

September

Planting in Early Fall is the Best for Plants

This is the second spring, in a sense, where you can get back out into the yard to sow grass seed and plant perennials and shrubs and trees. Also, now that the heat's broken, the plants come out of their summer-imposed dormancy and concentrate on growing once more. During drought and intense heat, plants divert their energy toward conserving water, which means they cut back on blooming or growing. That's why the roses all start blooming their heads off. And who can blame them.

A newly planted perennial in summer heat will curl up and wilt. This is because the summer heat is evaporating the water out of the plant faster than the roots can supply water to the leaves. Planting in the cool of fall, when the evaporation rate isn't as high, will keep the plant from going dry and wilting, and the plant can use its energy to send roots deep.

Nursery stock is now cheap. You can choose the trees with the best fall color instead of having to guess. Even among the same species you'll see variations in color and growth habit. Trees can be just as individual as people are.

Be a smart shopper. Look at the quality of the foliage and bark. Does the tree look happy, with plenty of healthy leaves and no bleeding spots in the bark? Beware of spotty leaves –

however, with many members of the rose family, such as crabapples and purple leafed plum, spots are almost inevitable.

Realize that many of the trees on display have been at the nursery for a long time -- some since spring -- and will consequently be potbound, roots winding around the inside of the pots. When planting the trees or shrubs, cut through the roots and fan them out so new roots will grow out and away from the tangle.

When you plant the tree, mulch it generously. Give it an inch of water weekly if there is no rain. That will get the tree ready for winter.

THE BOSS. A distinct variety introduced a few years since. Shape as shown in accompanying illustration. Skin is black green in color. Flesh deeply scarlet, unusually sugary, crystalline and melting. The rind is very thin and tough. It ripens early, and is enormously productive. This is considered by many the very best table melon for family use. Pkt., 5c.; oz., 10c.; ¼ lb., 25c.; lb., 85c.; 5 lbs. and over, 65c. per lb.

How to Weed When Weeds Have Taken Over Everything

If summer weeds have taken over your garden, it's easy to give in to despair. If only somebody would drive a brush hog through this mess! we cry.

However, the toughest part is getting started because it looks scary and impossible. But once you've started, often you find you're able to make enough progress to feel like you can finish it. Little by little, bit by bit is the key.

The most important thing to do is to make a dent in the garden. If you have a vegetable garden, then clear the rows with a weed-eater. Spray messy garden edges with non-selective weed killer. If you have a flower garden, then grit your teeth and start pulling or hoeing like crazy, even if it means losing a couple of plants.

Give yourself fifteen minutes to do the job. If you feel like working longer, then do so. In fact, you probably will.

Also, go after big weeds only. Don't bother with tiny weeds. You have to make a hole in the mess. Once you've made progress, your morale goes up, and you feel capable of tackling the whole thing.

Pumpkins!

It's pumpkin season again. Here are some tips for dealing with pumpkins and using them as decorations.

A pumpkin should be left on the vine as long as possible. Pumpkins can be harvested when the fruit stops growing, and when the skin has hardened and is all orange. Use a knife or garden clippers to carefully cut the pumpkin off, and give it about two inches of stem. Try to leave the vine otherwise undisturbed if there are other pumpkins on it.

When you pick up the pumpkin, pick it up by the sides, NOT by the stem. Sometimes, when the stem has been broken off, diseases can get into the pumpkin and then it turns to mush.

Sometimes the vine dies off before a pumpkin has completely ripened. You can get pumpkins to orange up a little if the weather cooperates. First, leave them on the vine if you can, but clear away any leaves or debris that might block the sun. If frost threatens, cover the pumpkin with clear plastic, anchoring it with rocks. If the day's a cool one, leave the plastic on all day. Temperatures in the 40's slowly but surely kill off pumpkins.

If you bring the green pumpkin into your house or onto the patio, be sure it gets plenty of sunlight and air circulation, and keep turning the green toward the light.

Wash your pumpkin off with a weak chlorine solution, using one cup of bleach to one gallon of water. Let the pumpkin dry off, then store it in a cool, dry place.

Don't store pumpkins on a cement floor because they tend to rot. Set them on a piece of cardboard instead.

When you choose a pumpkin to make a jack o' lantern, choose one that feels light for its size. There won't be so much meat on these, which makes carving easier.

Before carving, remember that a pumpkin will start to wither in two to four days, so plan accordingly. You might be able to revive a withered pumpkin by putting it in cold water for about eight hours. Put a little bit of bleach in the water to help stop decay.

When you're ready to carve, remember to set down plenty of newspapers or plastic sheeting to catch all the pumpkin brains!

Use an ice-cream scoop to take out the pumpkin seeds. Scrape the side that you're going to carve to about an inch thick to make your work easier.

After you carve the pumpkin, apply petroleum jelly to the cuts and to the entire inside of the pumpkin to prevent rotting and to make it last longer. Or store the pumpkins in large, plastic bags in a cool location to slow down water loss. (Be careful that you don't end up with moldy pumpkins, though.)

You might skip carving a face and simply take the top off the pumpkin. Then fill the pumpkin with late mums from the garden. If the pumpkin's large enough, you might be able to fit a small pot inside it. Then you can still plant the mums.

You can bake the seeds. Set them out to dry, then cook at 250 degrees for an hour with salt and a little melted butter, stirring them so they don't burn. Also, you can stir-fry them. Seeds are high in valuable vitamins and nutrients, not to mention that eating pumpkin seeds is a fun part of the whole pumpkin tradition.

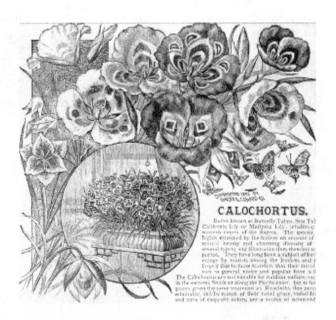

CALOCHORTUS.

Drying Fruit

My grandma tells me that her mom, Ruby, would dry apples by slicing them and laying them out on a sheet on top of one of the low outbuildings. She'd cover the sheet with cheesecloth to keep out the bugs. At the end of the day,

Ruby would take the sheet with the apples inside, and the next morning set the sheet out again. After several hot summer days, the apples were dried, and then she'd store them in jars.

I have a dehydrator, which is a great deal handier, especially since I don't have any outbuildings to put a sheet on top of.

Many books recommend that, before drying, you should dip apples in a solution of water and lemon juice to avoid discoloration. However, I have tried this and found that it actually takes longer to dry the apples after you get them wet. Imagine that. Also, the lemon juice didn't really make that much difference in the finished color of the apples. So now I skip that step, and they're dried in about nine hours.

Since I'm still waiting for my little apple tree to grow up, I go to the apple orchard and pick a great variety of apples – these are cheaper and the defects in the apples – sunscald, spots, minor bug bites – disappear once the apple is peeled. I like Golden Delicious, though nearly any apple variety would work.

Then I prepare them. Wash the apples, peel them, and then slice them with an apple slicer/corer – one of those things that you push down over the top of the apple. I try to keep the slices no more than a quarter-inch wide. Then I arrange them over each tray in the dehydrator. When all the trays are filled, run the dehydrator until the apples are dry and pliable, then store them in jars, tins, or plastic bags. If you have really wet, humid winters, stick them in the freezer.

The oven is also a good way to dry apples. Arrange the slices on cookie sheets and put them in. Turn the oven on to its lowest setting and leave the door cracked open. But you don't want to keep it more than 140 degrees in there. This method also works well, though it's a good idea to keep little kids out of the kitchen while this is going on.

If you want to reconstitute the dried fruit for cooking, soak them for about 12 hours. One pound of dried apples equals 3 ½ to 4 pounds of fresh.

Free Plants! Divide Your Perennials

I enjoy perennials for a number of reasons. You don't cripple your hands and wrists from planting millions of them every spring. In May, while annuals are still small and wimpy, perennials are already massive. Some perennials, such as candytuft, flax, irises, saxifrage, and columbines, are blooming before you can even get the annuals in the ground. Finally, when you need more perennials, all you have to do is divide the ones you already have.

Dividing perennials is generally more traumatic to the gardener than it is to the plant itself. Plants thrive after they've been divided – and you get all these free plants in the bargain. Also, undivided perennials stop blooming; once divided, they will start flowering again. You can't lose!

Perennials can be divided all fall, even into the winter. You should, however, try to get them divided several weeks before the ground freezes so the roots can get a little head start. The nice thing about dividing the plants in the fall is that they have all winter, and all next spring, to get established before the awful heat of summer hits.

Perennials need dividing if they have a large dead spot in the middle of the plant; if the plant has stopped blooming in the last few years; if the plant flops over when it used to stand up just fine; or if the plant looks crowded. Some perennials need dividing every few years, while some prefer less often.

Some shouldn't be divided at all, such as gas plant (*Dictamnus alba*), indigo (*Baptisia*), baby's breath, and columbines. Plants that are actually small woody shrubs shouldn't be divided either. These include candytuft (*Iberis sempervirens*), lavender, santolina, and artemesias.

Before dividing a plant, there are several things you should do. If the soil is dry, water the plants deeply a few days before you do the job. Dry roots are brittle roots, and dry soil will break apart, tearing the roots. By the same rule, see that the soil is not too wet, because digging while it is muddy ruins the soil structure.

Prepare the place where you're going to plant the divisions by digging some good, deep holes. Add bone meal, compost, or other good organic fertilizers to the soil and mix them in, loosening up the soil around the planting area as you do. It's a good idea to dig up any weeds in the area, too.

Give the plant the best soil you possibly can, and in return the plants will show you how happy they are.

Always have the holes prepared before you dig up the perennials. This way you get your plants into the ground immediately.

Then go to the perennials, shovel in hand. Clean up any dead leaves and stems around the plants. If the perennial is really big and tall, cut it back to a reasonable height.

My favorite method of dividing a plant is to dig up the plant's entire rootball. Then – and this is important – *put it back in the hole*. Make the dividing cuts by slicing into the plant with the shovel. If the plant is very tough and rootbound, I will jump onto the shovel to make the cuts. Then lever the separated plants out for transplanting.

I do this because rootballs tend to roll away when you attack them with a shovel. Also, when the plant's sitting in the ground, you can see the natural parts (as in the place where you *part* your hair) in the plant, and there's where you make the cuts. Sometimes this involves some fancy work with the shovel. Finally, the divisions stay cool and moist in the ground until you move them, instead of drying out in the sun.

Another way of dividing perennials is to stick two garden forks into the middle of the plant you're dividing. The forks should have their backs to each other and be close together. Then you use the forks to prize the plants apart. Once the crowns are separated, you can use a knife or some clippers to cut the roots apart.

If you want a lot of new plants and you don't care how small they are, you can shake off as much soil as you can and then just take the plant apart, making judicious cuts with the clippers. Daylilies, if not too overgrown, can be taken apart this way. You end up getting a half million tiny plants that won't look like much for a year. Plant them in some hidden spot in the garden until they get big enough to show off.

Some plants, like indigo (Baptisia), have very tough, woody crowns that you'll have to take a knife to. Chop it in half, or quarters, making sure each section has at least one or two eyes and roots.

Overcrowded irises might come out of the ground as one big plate. You can cut or break them apart; they don't seem to mind. Replant them shallowly, with the top of the rhizome under the fan of leaves sticking a little out of the soil. You end up with bags and bags of leftover rhizomes from this operation.

Peonies and other tuberous plants will need to be dug up and dunked in a bucket of water so you can find the buds on the tuber. Cut the tuber apart so each section will have several buds and roots, then plant. Peonies might not bloom the next year, but at least they'll get some good growing done.

Once you've divided them, discard any diseased or really wimpy-looking plants. Also discard the old centers, or crowns, of the plant.

If you do need to leave the new divisions out for a while, keep them shaded and protected from the wind until you can get them planted. If it's going to be several days, you might just dump them back in their old hole, cover them with mulch, and water them.

Plant the divisions in their new locations – please be sure to give each plenty of room to grow – and water them in well. Around the base of the plants, place a layer of newspapers, about five pages deep. Then pile about two or three inches of mulch over that. (Of course, if the plant is small, put down less mulch.) The newspaper will stop weed seeds before they can germinate, and keep the roots protected from the winter cold and from next summer's sun, and the mulch will make the area look nice and tidy. Give them a good drink every week, if you don't get an inch of rain, until it freezes. You might give the perennials a quart or two of water on temperate days through the winter if the season has been dry. Then you're set. Enjoy!

October

Tips for Preparing the Garden for Winter

In about 15 days, we are due for our first frost. Are you ready?

Start cleaning the vegetables out of the garden. Freeze, can, or dry what you have out there. I'm going to dry my tomatoes, carrots and peppers and make a winter soup mix out of it.

Herbs, too, can be frozen. Lay them out on a tray and put that in the freezer until they're solid. Then package them up, label them (ALWAYS label them!), and get them back in the freezer.

Keep tomatoes on the vines as long as you can. Pick off any small green tomatoes and all the flowers to allow the biggest green tomatoes to ripen. A tomato that's turning red when you pick it off the vine will go ahead and ripen. You can ripen green tomatoes by wrapping them in newspaper and letting them sit in a cool, dry place. You can also make fried green tomatoes.

Ditto with the peppers and the eggplants (though I wouldn't try fried green eggplant).

Leave parsnips in the ground, because frost improves their flavor by turning the starches into sugar. Carrots, too. Don't do this with potatoes, though – they will rot.

135

Wait for the vine to die before you pick a pumpkin. Also, the pumpkin should be the color you want it – like tomatoes, green pumpkins won't turn orange. Check the pumpkin with your fingernail. A ripe pumpkin will have developed a shell that your fingernail can't pierce.

When you cut the pumpkin off the vine, leave its stem on. If the stem comes off, let the scar dry before storing. Pick up the pumpkin by the bottom so the stem isn't pulled off.

Be sure to get the pumpkin in before night temperatures fall below 40 degrees.

To cure pumpkins, store them for 10 to 20 days in a cool place with good air circulation.

Don't store pumpkins with apples, because the apples give off a gas that make the pumpkins rot faster.

I've also been drying apples by the gallon. Some drying manuals recommend that you dip your apples into a lemon and water solution to keep them from browning when they dry. I found that the extra water on the apples slows down the drying time. I just slice the apples into pieces, throw them into the dehydrator, and switch it on. The apples don't brown very much at all (in fact, they look about the same as the apples I put through the lemon-water solution), and they dry in about nine hours.

MULTIFLORA BOUQUET ASTER

The Truth About Green Tomatoes

Last year I said that green tomatoes don't ripen. Some time later I received a letter that said they do ripen. I got the letter too late to run it, so I held onto the letter for a whole year, and what do you know, I didn't lose it!

Eudora Weldon of Graham, Mo., said, "I want to tell you green tomatoes will ripen. Wrap them in newspapers and store them in a cool place in a cardboard box. Check them in a few weeks. We have tomatoes until Christmas."

So you can do that. You can also make relish out of them, or piccalilli, or fry them up, just like in the book. I think I even remember reading, in one of the Little House books by Laura Ingalls Wilder, about Laura's mother using green tomatoes to make a mock-apple pie.

Winterize Your Lawn Mower

Gas shouldn't stay in the mower over the winter because it could jell and clog the carburetor. Run the mower until it completely runs out of gas. Or, you could add a fuel stabilizer to the gas in the tank if there's too much to waste in that way. After adding the stabilizer, run the mower for about five minutes to get the mixed gas through the machine.

Change the oil and filter on the mower so it's ready to go next spring. Also, this gives you a chance to check for contaminants in the system, if you know what you're looking for.

Clean up all parts of the mower. Have the blades sharpened and balanced. Clean out the deck while the blades are out, and all parts above deck, too, then set it out in the sun so it dries completely. Do the same for the bag that collects clippings. Tighten all nuts and bolts, and check all belts, safety shields, and filters. Spray all steel parts, including the blade, with penetrating oil.

If you have a reel mower, have a professional sharpen the blades on it.

Finally, store the mower in a dry place out of the rain. If you must store it outside, cover it securely with a waterproof tarp.

Late Fall Flowers

You can still plant stuff in your garden. Put in mums, pansies, and flowering kale for a little late-season color. Some of the cold-season plants can stay in the ground, too.

Snapdragons and alyssum will keep on giving you color, and will stay green through November, though they'll stop blooming. In the garden, you'll still have parsley, spinach, lettuce, and root vegetables, so don't pull everything up! Unless you really want to.

And of course there's still plenty of time to plant perennials, shrubs, and trees. Their roots will be in the ground, safe from winter's cold, and the roots will grow over the winter, though only a little bit. But when spring hits, these plants will pick right up and start growing, and you won't have to bother with all that spring mud and slush.

HARDY PERENNIALS

Tender Bulbs

Dig up tender bulbs like calla lilies, cannas, elephant ears, dahlias, gladiolus, etc. Separate the bulbs from the plants, let the bulbs dry out for a few days, then store them in dry peat moss in a dry, cool place, or keep them in paper bags. Be sure to label them so they don't get all mixed up next year.

FARFUGIUM GRANDE

Bringing the Houseplants Inside

My Missouri Department of Conservation calendar says that today is the average day of the first frost in northern Missouri. Have you brought your houseplants in?

Clean up a sunny area inside the house or garage where you plan to keep your houseplants through the winter. You might even clean the window and trim back any branches outside that block the sun. A south-facing location is best for the plants that have spent all summer outside. However, if your plants prefer shade, filter the light with a sheer curtain

Try to give the sun-loving plants as much sun exposure as you can. Though the winter sun is actually closer to the earth, the earth is tilted away from the sun, which drastically cuts down on the light's intensity (and this is also why the sun hangs so low in the south through the winter).

If you have large fluorescent lights, halogen lights, or metal halide lights, your houseplants will do just fine.

Even if you have good light for your plants, you will still see some leaves falling – especially if they're those little fig trees, which need a lot of light.

Before you bring the plants in, clean them off. Pick off all those dead leaves. Lift the rootball out of the pot and knock off any pillbugs that have made colonies on the roots. Take off the saucer if you can and clean it out, and clean the dirt off the outside of the pot.

Cut the plant back if it's tall and leggy, making your cuts above any buds that are leafing out. Rub aphids off the leaves, add potting soil to the pot if it needs it, and wash off the plant if the weather is nice. Spray the plant well with insecticidal soap to be sure you're not bringing in any unwanted guests.

If it's too cool to wash the plants outside, then put them in your tub to clean them up, and shake off the water before you take them out.

Once these plants have been brought in, keep a close eye on them for several weeks, to be sure they don't get taken over by aphids or other pests. You might spray them weekly with insecticidal soap to make sure the plants are clean. Be sure to get underneath the leaves.

Your asparagus fern will shed needle-like leaves constantly, so you'll need to vacuum under it a lot. (The leaves feel like needles when you step on them in your bare feet.) English ivy will need a soapy water bath every month to keep spider mites at bay. Move cactuses away from the window so the cold draft off the glass doesn't make them turn yellow.

To keep your houseplant leaves glossy and dust-free, wipe them with a cloth moistened with milk. To kill mealybugs and scale, dab them with a Q-tip moistened with rubbing alcohol.

Plants like high humidity, but humidity in winter houses is usually about 25 percent – the humidity level of the Sahara Desert. Keep plants in the bathroom, or grow them near a humidifier.

Another way to raise humidity is to fill a tray with aquarium gravel and a little charcoal. Then, fill the tray with water, and set the plants directly on the gravel. The gravel keeps the plant pots out of the water (so excess water can drain out of the pot) and the evaporating water keeps the air humid.

Houseplants Part 2: Now That They're Inside, Clean Them Up!

Now that your houseplants are safely inside for the winter, take a close look at them. Chances are that you have brought in some insect pests, or diseases, in with them.

If you haven't already, gently wash your plants with warm, soapy water to get rid of dust, insects, old leaves, and honeydew from the insects (honeydew is sugar water that insect pests secrete on the leaves). Be especially sure to wash under the leaves and along the stem. Rinse with plain water, then let them dry. Don't wash African violets or gloxinias; they resent this treatment. Brush the leaves instead.

Then check under the leaves and around the leaf stems for any unwelcome guests that like to hide out in these areas.

Spider mites are the hardest to spot, being only 1/50th of an inch long. These red or black mites spin tiny webs and suck the leaves' juices, sometimes making the leaf stippled or whitened. To discover them, shake the leaves over white paper -- the mites will fall on the paper and creep around.

Spider mites hate water and humidity, so keep the air moist around the plants. A good humidifier does wonders. Also, horticultural oil, or dormant oil, is a non-toxic way to smother them. Some plants, such as jade plant, blotch when they have this oil sprayed on them; check the label before you buy it.

Aphids are small pear-shaped bugs. They are colored green, brown and black. Some are winged and can fly to other plants. Not only that, they can lay eggs *and* give live birth without fertilization, so they multiply like something out of a B-movie. If you're not squeamish, you can rub them off a leaf or stem.

If you see ants on your plants, that is a sure sign you have aphids. Ants use aphids as honeydew "cattle," harvesting the sugar water off them. Set out ant traps and wash the plants to get rid of both.

Scale look like little brown water spots on the underside of leaves. The female lays eggs under her scale-like body, and then the nymphs creep away and find a permanent spot to sip plant juice, and end up sticking to the plant by their mouth parts. These are hard to detect, but honeydew – the sugar on the leaves – reveals their presence.

Mealybugs look like bits of cotton tucked into plant crevices. The cotton on their bodies is actually wax. If the mealybug infestation is small, dip a Q-tip in alcohol and touch it to each bug.

Whiteflies look like flying dandruff, and their nymphs look like tiny, waxy white scales, unmoving on the underside of leaves. The flying adults can be trapped by setting out yellow cards covered with stick-um like Tanglefoot or petroleum jelly.

Most of these insects can be controlled by keeping the plant clean through an occasional bath. However, if an infestation starts, get some insecticidal soap and add some rubbing alcohol to it. The alcohol penetrates the bug's protective waxy coating, allowing the soap to kill it. Spray this mixture weekly until the infestation is gone. Remember that some plants react badly to insecticidal soap, so check the label before you buy it. You can also get pyrethrum, which is an insecticide made from a type of daisy, to kill off the pests.

Fall Bug Attack! Boxelder Bugs, Ladybugs, and Crickets

In fall, you've probably noticed the bugs congregating on the south sides of houses, or magically appearing in older houses. Flies and other creatures also try to get into the house for a little warmth, only to meet a flyswatter. Just as well.

One of the congregating bugs are Asian ladybugs. These are different than the ladybugs you normally see in the garden. These ladybugs are larger and huskier, more of an orange color, and they are definitely more aggressive. Garden ladybugs have nibbled on my skin – I guess they wanted some protein – but their nibbling only tickles. When an Asian ladybug bites, it *hurts*.

In late fall, Asian ladybugs cover the sides of many houses. Like other congregating insects, they'll eventually go away when they crawl down into the leaves to try to survive the winter. Try not to kill them, because all ladybugs are quite helpful in the garden. It's when they get into the house that they're a problem.

If lots of beetles get inside, vacuum them up. However, you must immediately take the vacuum cleaner bag outside and empty it. If the beetles die inside the vacuum, they will smell up the vacuum and the house in short order. (A hand-held vacuum really comes in handy here – just take it outside and dump it out when you've vacuumed them up.)

Boxelder bugs also can be a problem this time of year. To get rid of them, spray them with detergent water. Use a car-wash attachment on your hose, or a sprayer -- or, after you've washed the dishes, throw the soapy water on them. This also cleans up your house.

If boxelder bugs get inside, they won't breed, so you don't have to worry about them infesting the house. They don't bite, either, nor will they harm anything.

Crickets, both the big black ones and the little brown ones, are another late-fall annoyance. Since they're are nocturnal creatures, they will chirp all night. When you turn on the light at 3 a.m. to look for them, the cricket immediately shuts up. You can move the stove and open all the cabinets, but you will not find them.

One way to catch a cricket is to set out a damp washcloth near where you heard it. The next morning, look for the cricket might be found in the folds of the washcloth.

Crickets like damp areas, which is why you see them in your gardening mulch after you water.

Another way to catch a cricket is to pour a little cornmeal in the middle of a glue trap and set it near the cricket's noise, preferably in a corner. The cornmeal should attract the cricket. (Put the glue trap out of the reach of the dog and cat, of course, unless you want to get awakened in the middle of the night by Fido jumping into bed with a glue trap stuck to his face.)

To keep ladybugs, boxelder bugs, and crickets from getting into the house in the first place, caulk any cracks on the outside of the house. Shut off all unnecessary lights around the house, or replace them with yellow lamps or sodium lights because crickets are attracted to bright lights. Also, keep weeds and plants short next to the house, and remove stacks of bricks or logs from next to the house. This will reduce the number of places these insects can hide and overwinter.

November

Orchids: Actually Not That Difficult To Grow (Mostly)

Orchids are often thought of as tough to grow and a kind of a prima donna. Well, maybe some of them are. But to grow an orchid is to get acquainted with one of the most fascinating plant species in the world.

Orchids are found all over the world, in trees in the rain forest, in prairies and forests, some near oceans or in deserts, some in the Arctic. There is an orchid that gets over 20 feet tall in Malaysia; there's one in Australia that's an inch tall, with flowers that are pinhead-sized. The real challenge is getting one to live in your house.

Before buying an orchid, look at what your home has to offer it. Can you provide the light and humidity your orchid needs? Humidity's a big factor. Orchids like 50% humidity ... while most winter homes have 20% -- less humidity than the Sahara Desert! Have a humidity tray for them – a low tray filled with pebbles. The pot sits on the pebbles, and then you fill the tray with water almost to the level of the pot. That usually does the trick.

It's best to buy orchids from plant shows, orchid growers, or from online. You might see some at chain stores, but be leery of them – the staff often doesn't know how to water them, so you end up buying orchids with root rot, and they don't survive.

Good orchids for beginners include Phaleonopsis, or the moth orchid; Cattleya, or the corsage orchid; and Oncidium, also called Dancing Lady.

The Phaleonopsis orchids are everywhere these days. If you can get them for under $10, that's a great price.

Orchids that like bright, sunny, and warm houses include Cattleya, Dendrobiums, and Oncidiums. Orchids that like indirect light include Phaleonopsis and lady slipper orchids.

I keep buying Phaleonopsis orchids when they're under $10. Oops. I keep them lined up in the windowsill at work where they get some sun. About every week, I'll stick them in the sink and run water that's slightly cool to the touch through their pots, wetting the wood chips in the pot thoroughly. Then I let the water drain out and then stick them back in their saucers in the window. That's it. Since the orchids are at the office, and I don't have much fertilizer handy (I keep forgetting to bring some), I give them a dose of weak coffee for fertilizer. They perk right up when I give this to them. It must be the caffeine! Though coffee does have other nice benefits for plants.

Next, choose your orchid, and be sure it's planted in the right soil (or soilless) mix. Epiphytic orchids prefer to grow in a loose bark mix, with a little leaf mold mixed in. This is usually what you'll see the Butterfly orchids grown in. Or grow them in crumbled charcoal or pebbles. Others have had success with coconut fibers or cork.

This soil mix won't provide a lot of nutrients to the plants, except for the leaf mold, so you'll have to add some fertilizer to the mix. They won't need a lot, maybe a dose every month or so. Be sure to flush water through the potting medium to be sure the salts from the fertilizer don't build up. You might also try giving your orchid a shot of compost tea occasionally. Put a little compost in a clear bottle, let it sit in the sun until the water looks like weak tea, then give the orchid a drink.

Since their home habitat is in treetops, with their roots in the air waiting for the next shower, then there should be plenty of air (and humidity) around the roots. No endophytic orchid should be standing in any water for any length of time! So, if water runs into the bowl underneath the pot, then empty the bowl out. Better yet, let the water run directly into the humidity tray underneath. Orchids should also be kept on the dry side.

If you're watering correctly, the orchid's roots will be white, firm, and fleshy. If you're doing it wrong, they'll be brown and squishy. Pretty straightforward.

Orchid roots might creep over the top of the pot. Don't repot it! Orchids just like to stick their feet out.

Plenty of light, plenty of humidity, take it easy on the water. Do that, and you should be fine.

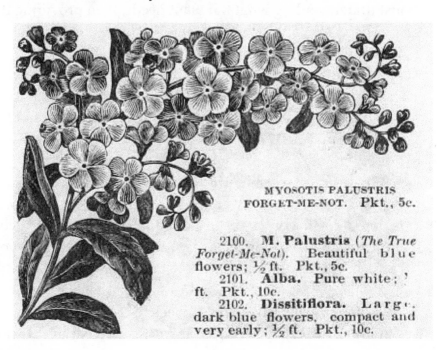

MYOSOTIS PALUSTRIS
FORGET-ME-NOT. Pkt., 5c.

2100. **M. Palustris** (*The True Forget-Me-Not*). Beautiful blue flowers; ½ ft. Pkt., 5c.
2101. **Alba.** Pure white; ? ft. Pkt., 10c.
2102. **Dissitiflora.** Large, dark blue flowers, compact and very early; ½ ft. Pkt., 10c.

How to Grow a Christmas Cactus Like Grandma's

I think that, in its day, a Christmas cactus was a required plant in every grandma's house, and most grandmas had a plant that was about the size of the living room. And every time you took a piece of the cactus home to start a new plant, it would just sit there and not grow. So you considered that proof that grandmas were actual miracle workers.

Christmas cactus is a tricky plant to grow – if you have the wrong conditions for it, that is. In the right conditions, the plant will grow big and happy with little effort. So it's just understanding what the plant needs, then providing it.

There are four types of this cactus – orchid, Easter, Thanksgiving (or crab), and the Christmas cactus. These plants are actual cactuses, but they are native to Brazil. In their native habitats, you'll find them growing in trees in the damp, humid rain forest. So if you've been withholding water from your Christmas cactus, then water it! Give it humidity, too.

These cactuses require care similar to orchids and bromeliads. They like porous, light soil mixed with leafmould. If you've been shredding leaves with your mulching mower, you'll have plenty of that. Or give your cactus a handful of rotted compost to cheer it up. Plants like that.

Water it generously once a week, but let the soil dry out slightly between waterings. The soil must drain quickly; overwatering rots the roots.

Right now flowers should be forming on the cactuses or (on the Thankgiving cactus) will be ready to bloom. When the cactus is preparing to flower, be sure to keep it watered.

Applying a little bit of water-soluble fertilizer, like MiracleGro, with each watering will help with blossoms.

Don't move the plant. These cactuses like to have 12 hours of darkness about this time and cool night temperatures (around 55 degrees); this helps to bring on the blossoms. Some will rebloom naturally about February.

After February, let the plant rest by cutting back a little on watering. Stop fertilizing until it starts putting out new growth. Anyway, too much chemical fertilizer will cause salt to build up in the soil. In April, when it starts growing again, try giving the plant a little compost tea to make it sit up and grow like crazy. Put compost and water in a bottle, set it in the sun to brew like sun tea, then dilute and water. Also, you might try this on a cactus cutting that refuses to grow. In May, put the cactus outside.

In high summer the plant will go into a heat-induced dormancy. (Technically, in high summer *everything* goes into a heat-induced dormancy.) Just keep it watered, give it shade, don't fret.

In September or October, bring the plant in, clean it up, and find a nice south window for it – and make sure it's a place where you can give it about 12 hours of dark every night. Start fertilizing it, and wait for the flowers.

Mealybugs like this plant – mealybugs are to cactus what blackspot is to roses. I've found that systemics or sprays don't do the job on these creatures. You know what does? Squishing them with your fingers. This is gross (even for me, and I've squished lots of bugs), but if you keep squishing them, infestations will eventually go away. A Q-tip dipped in rubbing alcohol and touched to each bug will also kill them off. Get underneath the stems, because mealybugs like to hide there.

Happy Thanksgiving, everybody!

Keep Bird Feeders Clean

Who ever thought a bird feeder could kill?

It's sad but true. Overcrowded bird feeders can breed diseases like salmonella and conjunctivitis – a kind of pinkeye found mostly in house finches, which causes the eyes to crust shut. Birds, unable to see, become lunch for a predator. Overcrowded bird feeders can also lead to a disease like aspergillosis, which is caused by breathing mold spores from old seed. The disease leads to bronchitis and pneumonia, and in some cases can lead to death. Rancid suet in suet feeders can also make birds sick.

As you clean the kitchen table and the floor underneath, so must you clean the bird feeders. Do this every week, and the birds will bless you for it.

First, put on gloves to protect yourself against diseases. Then take down the feeder and dump out old seeds away from the feeding station. Any debris on the ground below the feeder should be shoveled up and disposed of in the same fashion.

Scrub the feeder with hot, soapy water. If it's dishwasher-safe, send it on a solo run in the dishwasher. Once the feeder is clean, rinse it with a freshly-made solution of one part of bleach to nine parts of water. Let it air-dry; don't rinse the bleach off. Also, don't use vinegar as a substitute for bleach, because vinegar is not a disinfectant. Then refill the feeder with fresh seed or nectar – only a small amount, so less is wasted – and put it back up.

Never feed the birds moldy seed or bread. Always store birdfeed in waterproof containers in a cool, dry place.

Every year, move your feeder a few feet away from its old place to allow last year's bird mess to be absorbed by the soil – and to keep last year's diseases from recurring.

The birdbath will require similar treatment. Rinse the birdbath out daily. Every week, scrub it with detergent and a bristle brush. Twice a month, fill it with a 1:10 bleach/water solution, pour it out, let it air-dry, then rinse well before refilling with water. Clean heating elements as well.

If your feeder or birdbath is crowded, get a second one and set it up a good distance from the first. Crowded conditions lead to more disease for everyone.

You might also consider buying a water-warming device to keep the birdbath from freezing. This time of year, birds (and all other animals) need water so badly, and that would help them so much.

If at any time you should see a dead bird near the feeder, bury the bird. Clean the feeder and the area around it, then move it to a different location in your yard. Don't take it down altogether, because diseased birds that frequent your feeder will head to other feeders, spreading the disease to different birds.

Don't try to capture sick birds. Some bird diseases can be transmitted to humans. Also, some birds, such as those with conjunctivitis, will recover on their own. Capturing them will send them into shock, and this will not help matters very much.

I actually caught a bird with conjunctivitis. My daughter and I were hiking at the top of the hills at Squaw Creek when I came across a female house finch whose eyes were stuck shut from pinkeye. I felt so bad for her, as she was completely blind. I caught her. What I should have done was stick her in my pocket and zip it shut. Instead I tried to go down the steps while carrying the bird in my hands. A mistake. She broke free and fluttered high, high over the hills, then circled blindly down, unable to see where she was going, until she disappeared into the trees. I don't know if I could have done anything to help her, but I was sad that she was on her own. It was just one little bird, but still.

With a clean feeding area for the birds, you can take pride in knowing that you're doing your part to make life less harsh for your friends.

December

'Tis the Season for ... Poinsettias

Did you know that poinsettias are one of the most popular Christmas plants in the nation, and that approximately 63 million pots of them have been sold in one six-week period? You can get the red ones, of course, but there are also poinsettias with cream, white, pink, or (rarely) purple bracts. Some look as if they'd been speckled with bleach, which makes an interesting effect. Some have leaves that curl back on themselves. But don't buy those with powdery white spots on the leaves and bracts. That's not decoration, it's powdery mildew.

Okay, everybody, say it with me: Poinsettias are not poisonous. Many poinsettia nurserymen have eaten poinsettia leaves to show, "Look, these things will not kill you!" They survived that, only to be finished off by all the insecticides sprayed on the plants while in the greenhouse. Just kidding! (Partly.)

But these nurserymen who eat the leaves report that the leaves are bitter and taste awful, which should deter the toddlers. Also, a 50-pound kid would have to eat about 500 to 600 leaves before they get toxic. Basically, the dangers of the poinsettia are these: that eating leaves will give you a tummy-ache, and that some people may experience skin irritation from the milky white sap. So fear not.

When selecting a poinsettia, look for plants that have tightly-closed flowers. (You probably already know that the red "petals" are actually modified leaves, or bracts, while the true flowers are the tiny clusters of anthers in the center of the bracts.) If the poinsettia's true flowers are open and showing pollen, then the bracts won't last as long as one in which the flowers are still closed.

Avoid plants sold in sleeves – paper, mesh, it doesn't matter – because the sleeves restrict air flow around the leaves, resulting in an unhappy-looking plant when you get it home and unveil it. However, you must wrap up the plant before you take it to your car to avoid cold damage.

Look for green, healthy foliage clear down to the soil line. Don't buy plants with green around the edges of the bracts. Beware of wilted plants with wet soil; these may have root rot and are not long for this world. The poinsettias on display should not be close to the door, since these plants cannot stand temperatures below 50 degrees.

When you get them home, keep them away from windows, drafts, and high heat (definitely don't place them next to a wood stove). They like their room temperature to be about 68 to 72 degrees, which is easy. Give them lots of sunlight. Water them well, but empty out any extra water in their saucers, and let them dry out slightly between waterings. They're like peace lilies, in that they'll droop when they really want water, but once they get a drink they'll spring right back. Just don't let them droop all the time, since that does stress out a plant.

Wait until after the bracts fall off to fertilize the plants.

Most people say that it's better to just toss out the poinsettias after they're done blooming, because home-bloomed plants don't look as spectacular as the ones you get from greenhouses. However, I'm a piker and hate to throw out plants. Also, I think the dark-green foliage is interesting in itself through the year – more interesting than, say, a schefflera, which I consider to be a positively boring plant. So you make the call.

Josephine, Empress of the Roses

Reading an heirloom rose catalogue can end up being a short study in French. Madame Isaac Pereire. Fantin-Latour. Blanc Double de Coubert. Souvenir de la Malmaison. Why are so many old roses crowned with French names?

It's because roses owe a debt to the Empress Josephine.

Josephine was born in Martinique, in the West Indies, where her given name was Rose. She was known as the "Bird of the Islands" because of her love of Martinique's flora and fauna. She ended up in France, married to Alexandre de Beauharnais. During the Reign of Terror in the French Revolution, both were imprisoned. Beauharnais was guillotined, and Rose was doomed. But a month later, with Robespierre's execution, the Reign of Terror was over. Rose was released from prison, destitute, but she quickly used her influence to regain some property. She soon found her place in society again, and she met Napoleon, who fell in love and renamed her Josephine.

After their marriage, while Napoleon was creating his empire, Josephine purchased a country estate outside of Paris named Malmaison. This was in 1799. She began to gather, from all around the world, the choicest plants, animals, and artwork that she could find. She drew on her Martinique home for inspiration for her gardens. Napoleon helped. During his military campaigns across the world, he had his troops send plants and seeds to Malmaison. Reportedly, he even brought seeds of Egyptian poppies back in his boots.

'It is a joy for me', she said in 1804, 'to see foreign plants multiply in our gardens. In ten years time I want to see that every French department owns a collection of precious plants initially grown in our nurseries'.

Josephine had a conservatory built for her tropical collection. Scientists from all over Europe came to admire her almost unparalleled collection of rare plants and flowers. Professors at the National History Museum in Paris collaborated with her.

And nothing stood in Josephine's way when she wanted plants. At one point during the Napoleonic Wars, Napoleon blockaded the French coast against British goods. Despite that, Josephine had plant cuttings shipped in from several

British nurseries. And she figured a cashmere shawl or two wouldn't make that much difference! Napoleon probably paid the bill for that, too.

Josephine's rose collection at Malmaison was outstanding. She had decided to grow every available species of rose available. With Napoleon's help she gathered 250 species of rose. She hired botanists to work with her collections. This was about the time that Mendel's work with genetics came to light, so the botanists were able to make crosses that created new rose varieties.

Even after Josephine died in 1814, her work lived on. Many gardens sprang up around Europe and America in the style of the gardens of Malmaison. It helped that Josephine had been generous; all one had to do was ask her for plant cuttings and she'd send them.

Rose breeding exploded in France. A catalogue from 1791 lists only 25 rose varieties; one from 1829, just 40 years later, lists 2,562. One of the new roses was "La France," the first hybrid tea – the ancestor of the hybrid teas we have today.

After Josephine's death, and in the days before his exile, Napoleon walked the gardens of Malmaison one last time. He stopped before a garden of roses, and, overcome by emotion, said, "Poor Josephine! I cannot accustom myself to living here without her. I seem always to see her coming along the path, gathering one of these flowers which she loved so well. Truly she was the most graceful woman I have ever seen."

Water Does Not Equal Love for Houseplants

Whether you grow calla lilies or one of those tiny bromeliads you can buy in a shell as big as a quarter, the houseplants are going to need water. But not too much!

Now, many people equate water with care: "If I water my plant, I am caring for it." This is good. However, many people water the plant daily, or water when the plant doesn't need it, or water plants in containers with no drainage holes. In these cases, water equals death to the plant.

Plant roots need oxygen, just as leaves do. So, if roots sit in water, they rot. If your plant has been overwatered in the past, then let the plant dry out and vow never to overwater again. Then stick to that vow.

So how do you keep from overwatering? Granted, a spathiphyllum, or Peace Lily, will need more water than a cactus, and it will do one spectacular fainting act if you don't give it water. So to keep from getting confused, there are a few rules of thumb.

The main rule: always check the soil before you water! Some pots or potting soil hold water better than others. A sandy soil will hold less water than a peat-based soil mix. Stick your finger into the soil about an inch deep and see how soggy the soil is. Do this every time you water.

Some people also use little watering indicators that you stick it in the soil. If the plant has enough water, the little watering pot is green; but if you need to water, the pot turns yellow. However, these stop working after a few months.

Generally, I water plants once a week, but only if they need it. If the plant is blooming or setting buds, I'll water a little more often to keep up the plant's strength. When it's winter, I'll water less. Avoid frequent light watering; a good drink when the soil's a bit drier is best for most plants.

Sometimes it's hard to know when to water, because often the top of the soil will look positively parched, when in fact the soil's perfectly moist a half-inch down. In my amaryllis pot, I'm experimenting with a method that seems to work pretty well: I set a shell in the pot, nestled into the soil. To check if the plant needs some water, I lift up the shell and look at the soil under it, comparing it to the soil around the shell.

You can easily see if the soil's moist or dry under the shell. It seems to work pretty well, especially with those deceptive peat soil mixes that always look dry.

Some plants prefer different watering methods. Bromeliads should have water poured directly into the vase its leaves make. Orchids like light watering and lots of humidity. Plants in the African violet family should be watered in the saucer, not from the top, because the plants are prone to leaf-spotting and crown rot. Let the plant stand in the water-filled saucer for about a half hour, then pour the water off, since they hate wet feet.

Fertilizers such as Miracle-Gro in the water help the plants, since frequent watering leach the nitrogen out of the soil. But fertilize only once a month. Using fertilizer every time you water the plants builds up salt in the soil, which eventually kills the plant.

How to Buy a Great Gardening Book

Whether you're buying a gardening book as a gift or for yourself, it's important to get the best book for your buck. This is difficult because of the sheer number of books cascading from publishing houses.

When you read enough gardening books (this applies to books in any field, whether it's writing, finance, cooking, etc.), you start seeing the same information over and over. What you need to find are books that have new angles on the subject, new information, and new ways of looking at things.

It helps if a gardening boss recommends the book, or if other gardeners say, "You've got to read this!" Word of mouth is a super help in finding new books to enjoy. But when you don't have a recommendation, you've got to figure it out on your own. Here's how.

First, find out what the book offers. Read the flap copy and the blurbs on the back. Then scan the table of contents. (Sometimes that's enough to stop you right there.) Then, buzz through the body of the book to see if you like what you see – the writing style, how advanced the information is, and whether can you apply this book to your own garden or not.

Are there good illustrations or photos, with captions that tell you what you're looking at? Sometimes the pictures are pretty but there's no meat in the text. Can you understand what the author is saying? Is the author trying to obfuscate the meaning just to make himself sound important? Those books I throw aside.

One important thing to check for is a bibliography. Flip to the back of the book and see what books the author's referred to in her research. I like an author who does her research. If a book doesn't have a biblio, then I have to wonder if the research in the book is any good.

Another thing to check for is hands-on work. Has the author had actual experience in the topic she's writing about, or has she interviewed people who has? It's one thing to sit in your cushy chair and type stuff about xylem and phloem, but it's another thing to get hit in the head with a tree limb full of xylem and phloem because you didn't duck fast enough when you cut it off the tree. Also, a hands-on gal is going to experience the book in a way that somebody sitting around in an office never does. Out in the field, you find out real quick what works and what doesn't.

The last thing to watch out for in the gardening book section are British imports that are trying to pass themselves off as American. These aren't so bad, but if you grab a Brit book without realizing it and try to apply it to your garden, you find that some of the information throws you. Say, you go out and plant the flowers the book discusses, then find out later that the only place these plants can prosper in the States is in the Pacific Northwest, where the weather's similar to England's.

Tips-offs that the book is British: they talk about your soil being chalky or peaty. They use words like *fertiliser*, *Pelargoniums* (for geraniums) and *centre*. They feature a lot of acid-soil plants like heath, heather, and strawberry trees. I wish!

Dead giveaway the book is British: any mention of hedgehogs.

Samples from Some of My Other Gardening Books!

If You're a Tomato, I'll Ketchup With You: Tomato Gardening Tips and Tricks.

The National Gardening Association has found that, among vegetable gardeners, tomatoes are their favorite plant to grow. One in three Americans have a vegetable garden, and 9 out of 10 of those gardens have tomatoes in them.

Welcome to the world of tomato gardening.

There's nothing as sweet and good as a sun-warmed tomato fresh from the garden on a hot summer afternoon. It's no wonder that tomatoes are the most popular vegetable in America (though botanically, tomatoes are a fruit). Cordell's book walks you through the steps in raising tomatoes – through starting tomato seeds, planting (and tricks for planting tomatoes early), and staking and caging tomatoes. Readers learn how to fight off diseases and insect *pests, decipher the mysterious letters on a tomato tag, how to harvest tomatoes, and how to dry, can, or freeze tomatoes for next year.*

With plenty of information for advanced gardeners, ready help for beginning gardeners, lots of expert knowledge, and a smidgeon of wit, If You're a Tomato will guide you in the ways of the vegetable garden with a minimum of fuss and feathers. And also with a minimum of weeding. Nobody likes weeding.

Tomato Varieties

The National Gardening Association has found that, among vegetable gardeners, tomatoes are their favorite plant to grow. One in three Americans have a vegetable garden, and 9 out of 10 of those gardens have tomatoes in them.

In January and February, when spring fever is really hitting hard, those heirloom seed catalogs inspire dreams of the perfect vegetable garden and the veritable cornucopia of delicious vegetables that it will pour upon our collective tables. Not literally of course, as that would be a mess. But man, those seed catalog tomatoes. It wouldn't be so bad if the seed catalogs could offer taste samples of everything.

When I flip through the Baker Creek seed catalog, which is far and away my favorite, they offer 13 pages of tomatoes (and one page of tomatillos). And so many heirloom varieties. Who knew there was such a variety of tomatoes? Green tomatoes, orange tomatoes, pink tomatoes. Here are the purple, black, and brown tomatoes, which include Black Krim, Cherokee Purple, Paul Robeson, and True Black Brandywine. They have red tomatoes, naturally, two pages of striped tomatoes, two pages of Brad Gate's multicolored tomatoes, some of which are downright psychedelic in purples, yellows, reds, and browns. Then we have blue tomatoes (actually rich purples) and white tomatoes (a very pale yellow, as if Bunnicula had been at work on them), and of course yellow tomatoes. I had a Yellow Pear tomato plant that took over half my garden. I can appreciate that kind of vigor in my plants. You can also get peach tomatoes, which have a light layer of fuzz.

Tomatoes also range in size from gigantic beefsteak tomatoes that can weigh up to a half-pound, to the smallest cherry tomato about the size of a marble. You can grow heavy-yielding hybrids or open-pollinated heirloom varieties in different colors, shades, and sizes. You can choose early varieties that set fruit when it's cool outside, mid-season varieties, and late-maturing varieties that will give you the biggest fruits but take 80 to 90 days to do it. Sometimes you'll need about 120 days to get a decent harvest, but hey, at least you get tomatoes!

Tomatoes are so versatile and so good. You can cook them a million different ways or you can eat them, sun-warmed and delicious, straight off the vine. Some people grab a cherry tomato, a leaf of basil, and a slice of mozzarella cheese, and eat them like that.

Yellow Pear tomatoes, an heirloom variety, and also an indeterminate tomato. I had a Yellow Pear tomato plant once that took over the whole garden. It was great.

Determinate vs. indeterminate

I've known about these two different kinds of tomatoes for decades and yet I still can't keep them straight in my head. It's like the difference between flammable and inflammable, kind of.

Determinate tomatoes produce fruit at the ends of their branches. These will stop growing when they are still pretty short.

Indeterminate tomatoes bear fruit along their stems, which keep growing and growing and growing.

If you want a little short tomato to grow in a pot on your patio, get a determinate one.

If you want a Godzilla tomato to take over the world, get an indeterminate one.

Starting Tomatoes from Seed

If you start tomatoes from seed, it's best to start them inside, whether on a window sill or in a cold frame. At any rate, tomatoes need a soil temperature of at least 60 degrees to germinate, though they prefer warmer temperatures, up to 80 degrees. It's a sure bet that your outdoor soil temperature aren't going to get that high any time soon!

Tomato seeds need to be started six to eight weeks before the last frost date.

You can start Early Girl tomatoes (or any early tomato variety) under lights as early as February, then, when the weather is mild enough, transplant to the garden with a Wall o' Waters to help protect the plants against all the frosts.

Traditionally, in Missouri, zone 5, this date has been May 15. With global warming as it is, that date can be moved back to May 1, and even earlier. (Old gardening wisdom is always helpful, but still needs to be updated from time to time.)

So get out your calendar and count back six or eight weeks from your frost date, and that's your sowing date. (Protip: Keep a gardening calendar and notebook where you

175

write down things like sowing dates, the dates you see frost, etc., and use them next winter when you're planning for the next planting year.)

Next, line up your planting containers. Whether you use old egg cartons, Solo cups, flower pots, have them scrubbed (well, don't scrub the egg cartons) if you're reusing them. (Cleaning up the trays/flower pots will clean up any diseases that might be harbored there – diseases that could affect your young seedlings. Use hot water, soap, and a dash of bleach.)

Be sure that, whatever you use, your planter has plenty of drainage holes! This is not negotiable!

For seeds, it's best to use a light seeding mix that is high in vermiculite, though not necessary. A regular "soilless" potting mix is fine. The seeding mix, which is more expensive, also is lighter and easier for newly-germinated seedlings to poke their little green heads through.

When I ran a greenhouse, I started my seedlings in trays and then transplanted them to six packs and four packs later on when they were big enough. For small windowsill operations, this won't be necessary. You can put some soil in a small Solo cup (with drainage holes poked into the bottom), stick two or three tomato seeds in there, and let 'em grow until they're big enough to transplant directly into the garden.

The tomato seeds will germinate more effectively if you have a heat mat under the cups or trays. This will warm the soil with dependable heat, allowing the seedlings to germinate more quickly and grow out more quickly. Just be sure to get a thermostat with the mats so you can adjust the temperature so you don't end up cooking your seeds.

How to plant tomato seeds

Fill your pots, cups, etc. with potting mix, leaving about a half-inch to an inch at the top. Poke two seeds into the middle, about a quarter-inch deep, and cover them. Two seeds are just insurance, just in case one doesn't sprout. When they get bigger, pinch out the wimpier seedling and let the larger one grow.

Gently pack the soil in around the seeds, as seed-to-soil contact is very important for good germination rates.

Sprinkle water on the soil, and keep the soil moist. Don't let it dry out, and don't let it get soggy all the time. Having the soil dry out will kill the seedlings, and constantly wet soil will rot them.

Now one way to keep the soil from drying out is to cover the trays or pots with plastic wrap. This is an easy way to keep the soil moist.

If you use plastic wrap, don't leave the trays in direct sunlight. One time I had the soil covered this way on one of my flats. I came in from one of my jobs and realized that it had been sitting in the sun all afternoon. I ran over and lifted up the plastic wrap – and steam puffed out. Those seeds were roasted!

Once the seeds germinate, though, be sure to remove the plastic wrap, and also have a small fan to keep the air circulating a little around them. Seedling are susceptible to a disease called "damping off" which is encouraged by poor air circulation.

Damping-off disease

I had a bout of damping-off disease in my greenhouse, and it was a mess. Damping-off is a fungal disease that causes newly-planted seedlings to keel over and melt away.

It spreads out in a circle, as most funguses do (consider "fairy rings," which are circles of mushrooms on the forest floor), killing off seedlings as it spreads outward.

I haven't had damping-off before, since I keep stuff more on the dry side in the greenhouse, which the fungus doesn't like. However, we had cloudy, cold weather for a whole week, and my trays of seedlings, watered on a Sunday, would not dry out for the rest of the week. No sun, and I couldn't turn on the fans to pull the air through because it was too cold. Humidity was high. All the conditions were right for the fungus to strike.

Then the disease got into the snapdragons I'd just planted and started knocking them out everywhere. I called everyone I could think of for help. Then I took their advice, and it worked.

The best defense is a good offense. Keep a fan running at all times to keep the air circulating. You should feel the air moving through the whole room, but you don't have to turn it up so high that it blows the mice out from under the floor. Keep the plants spaced apart to let air move between them. The fungus likes high humidity and temperatures about 70 degrees. The fan keeps the humidity and temperature lower.

This will break your heart, but get rid of everything that's been infected by the fungus. Dump out the soil and the plants with them, and take the waste outside so spores won't reinfect the plants. As soon as you see the plant keel over, and you know it's not due to being underwatered, out it goes.

If it's a really valuable tray of seedlings, you might dig out the infected plants, isolate the tray from all the other plants, and try a soil drench of Captan fungicide (follow label directions). However, don't bank on saving the seedlings.

Hardening off the seedlings

Once the seedlings get big and husky, and once the weather warms up outside, it's time to harden off the seedlings so they can get acclimated to the weather outside. Plants do better if they have a little time to adjust to the cold temperatures, and the sun, and the wind.

About a week or two before you plan on planting them outside, start moving them outside for a little while. On the first couple of days, water them, then set them outside in the shade in a protected, warm area for an hour or two, then bring them back inside. Then slowly increase exposure to the sun and wind, leaving them out three hours, or four. Then, when you are close to planting time, leave them outside overnight several times (but only if the temperature is supposed to stay over 50 degrees all night).

While you're hardening them off, keep an eye on them to make sure they're not wilting or drying out.

When they're inside, reduce the amount of water you give them, and don't fertilize them until you plant them in the garden.

Don't worry if you miss a day, and don't stress about "not doing it right." Plants are often tougher than we give them credit for, and often there's no real "right way" or "wrong way." Sometimes regular life gets in the way, so if you can't put your seedlings out every single day, it's okay, just put them out when you can.

Now a sample chapter from my book on roses: _Rose to the Occasion: An Easy-Growing Guide to Rose Gardening_.

Roses are the Queen of Flowers. They're beautiful, fragrant, and elegant - and roses require all the pampering of a real Queen, don't they?

Actually, they don't!

Rose gardening can be easy and pleasant. I've worked 25 years in horticulture and cared for over 300 roses in a public rose garden when I was municipal horticulturist. I found ways to keep rose gardening fussbudgetry to a minimum while growing vigorous roses that bloomed their heads off. Rose to the Occasion: An Easy-Growing Guide to Rose Gardening shares tricks and shortcuts that rosarians use, plus simple ways you can keep up with your to-do list in the rose garden.

Gardeners of all skill levels will find this book helpful, whether they be beginning gardeners or old rosarians, whether they have a green thumb or a brown thumb.

Rose to the Occasion is the ultimate resource for any rose gardener, or anybody in need of good gardening advice. Roses are filled with romance, history, color, and fragrance. Grow some. They are worth it.

INTRODUCTION

When I started working as city horticulturist, I took care of a bunch of gardens around the city, including the big Krug Park rose garden. It included a bunch of the usual scrawny tea roses, some shrub roses, and a bunch of bare ground.

At the time I was more of a perennials gal, but when I looked at the roses, some of them were really nice. The 'Carefree Delight' roses were covered with rumpled pink blossoms. There was a tall 'Mr. Lincoln' rose and some 'Double Delights' that smelled amazing. A bunch of 'Scarlet Meidilands' were really putting on a blooming show, with tiny scarlet flowers cascading all over them. Not shabby at all.

I started taking care of the roses, but I noticed that a lot of the 'Scarlet Meidilands' were sprouting odd growths. Most of the new growth looked fine, with bronzed, flat leaves that looked attractive. But some of the new growth was markedly different – skinny, stunted leaves with pebbled surfaces, and hyperthorny canes that were downright rubbery. The blossoms on these shoots were crinkled and didn't open worth a darn.

I hollered at Charles Anctil, a Master Rosarian with the American Rose Society. We'd known each other since 1992 when we both worked at the Old Mill Nursery. He'd been working with roses for a good 50 years, and he knows his stuff. At any rate, Charles looked over the roses and told me that those roses, and others, had rose rosette virus, a highly contagious disease, and a death sentence for a rose. Every one of those roses had to come out. He couldn't believe the extent of the damage. He said that he had never seen so many roses infected by rose rosette in one place.

Oh great! Why do I get to be the lucky one?

'Evelyn' rose, a lovely rose from David Austin, a rose breeder who mixes the best of the old roses with the best of the new roses.

I dug up many roses that spring. That winter, I got a work crew and dug up 50 more. I had to replace all those roses, so I started researching new varieties.

As city horticulturist with no staff, I was already running like hell everywhere I went, so I wanted roses that wouldn't wilt or croak or wrap themselves in blackspot every time I looked at them cross-eyed. I wanted tough roses, roses that took heat and drought and bug attacks and zombie apocalypses with aplomb and would still come out looking great and covered with scented blossoms. (And the blossoms HAD to be scented – there was no two ways about that.)

I started reading rose catalogs. I talked to Charles some more, which is always fun. Somewhere along the way, I got obsessed. I immersed myself in roses. That's how I learn – I get excited about a subject and start reading everything in sight about it, as if it's a mini-course in school. I read about antique roses, which were making a comeback. Different rose breeders, most notably David Austin, were crossing modern varieties with old varieties and to get roses that combined the best of the new and the old. Other breeders were creating roses that were tough and disease-resistant, such as the 'Knock-Out' landscape rose, which now you see everywhere.

I planted some antique roses, and they looked great. I planted more. The rose garden was starting to look spiffy, even though I still had to take roses out every year due to the rose rosette virus. I even tucked in some annuals and perennials around the garden to doll up the place when the roses conked out in July and August.

Roses are amazing plants. Many old roses have a long and storied history. Some species that were growing during the time of the Pyramids are still blooming today. And these roses are attractive and fragrant. What could be better?

Some people say that you can't grow roses organically. I say you can. I did use a few chemicals when I was a horticulturist, but that was because I had a huge list of things to do in a limited amount of time. I used Round Up for spot-weeding (a tiny squirt for each weed, just enough to wet the leaves), a systemic granular fungicide to keep up with blackspot, and Miracle-Gro as part of the fertilizing regimen for convenience.

If you choose to use chemicals, use them responsibly. Don't spray them and expect the problem to be fixed. They work best when you combine them with other control methods. I'll give you an example that's not rose-related. I had a mandevilla plant in the greenhouse that had a huge mealybug problem. (Mealybugs are a small, white insect that sucks out plant juices. The young bugs look like bits of cotton.) I sprayed the plant with insecticide until the leaves were dripping. The mealybugs were still there. I put a systemic insecticide around the roots of the plant and watered it in. The mealybugs didn't care.

So I just started squishing the mealybugs with my fingers, a gross job because they squirt orange goo. At that point, I didn't care. I searched them out and squashed them where they were cuddled up around buds, in the cracks of the plant, and under the leaves. I even found some on the roots just under the soil. I squished those and added a little extra potting soil. I checked the plant every other day and squished every mealybug I could find. After a while, I stopped finding them altogether. Then I fertilized the plant, and the mandevilla put out leaves like crazy and started blooming. Success!

Chemicals aren't a cure-all by any means. They're convenient, but sometimes you just have to get in and do a little hands-on work with the plant to help it along. It's a good feeling when a plant you've been working with rights itself and perks up again.

Though I'm no longer a horticulturist, I wrote this book because I have worked in horticulture for about half my life, and have a decent understanding about how the natural world works. I might possibly be just a little crazy about roses. I hope my experiences are helpful and that you're able to benefit from them – and that your roses benefit as well.

The end of the sample!!

If you like this chapter, you can find the whole <u>ebook of Rose to the Occasion here</u>!

Perennial Classics: Planting & Growing Great Perennial Gardens

Perennials are the backbone of the garden -- a low-maintenance, long-growing mainstay that the garden revolves around. I've worked with perennials for 20 years, as a manager in the perennials section at the local nursery, and then as a municipal horticulturist in charge of over 20 gardens around the city. I've grown perennials from seed, potted them bare-rooted, divided them, deadheaded them, treated them for diseases and pests. Everything I've learned over the years I share here in this book -- Perennial Classics.

INTRODUCTION

WHY ARE PERENNIALS HARD TO BEAT?

When I was in college, I hit a rough patch and had to drop out. I was working two part-time jobs while taking full-time classes, paying for rent, food, and college (I had no financial aid), while living on ramen and hot dogs. (Fun fact: Due to my poverty diet, the iron levels in my blood were so low that I was not allowed to give blood.) Also, I kept wanting to change majors – I wanted to be an English major, but I kept being told that I needed to get a major that I could earn money in. "You can't make a living out of writing books." So I came back home and started living in my old hometown of Nodaway, and I got a job at a garden center.

I had a great boss and co-workers at the garden center. We worked with the annuals, perennials, and herbs. We would sing while grooming the plants (when I say "grooming the plants," I mean picking the dead leaves and old flowers off the plants – we weren't brushing the plants' hair or anything). We had a lot of good stuff to talk about, and we helped customers find what they wanted, and when they had gardening questions and we didn't know the answers, we'd do everything we could to find the answer. It was a great deal.

The nice thing about working at a garden center is that you get a lot of free plants. Every day you'd work through the flats and pots, and if you saw any plants that were dying or droopy or looked bad, you'd take them out. Some of them just needed a little tender loving care, so those would go to the "plant hospital," as we called it, where they would get a little attention and to perk up. Some of these would recover enough to go back on the tables, but some just sat there looking mopey, so we got to take these home.

I had a bit of a garden where I lived, but now I had a lot of garden. I wasn't very interested in annuals, because they were there for a season and that was it for them. But I loved the perennials. After all these years, I'm trying to put my finger on why they appealed so much to me. I think it was because everybody grew the same annuals over and over – marigolds, geraniums, petunias – but perennials weren't as common. I always go for stuff that's a little uncommon.

Another part of it was that some of these perennials could be true heirlooms in the garden, growing for years and years. I really wanted to grow a Gas Plant (*Dictamnus albus*) because they could stay alive for decades. Alas, the ones we had were just not in very good shape, and I didn't have much luck getting them started in my garden.

At the time, too, I was a little tired of the sameness of all the annuals. Granted, I would change my mind later, when I was working as a city horticulturist, because annuals were such a help in coloring up my flower beds fast. But give me a break, I was in college, and at that time I was just a teeny bit pretentious. Okay, more than a teeny bit.

Blister Beetles: The black is the most common; it feeds upon the flowers. Daily hunting and shaking the beetles into a pan of kerosene will quickly

I also loved the variety of perennials. I had some Connecticut Blue delphiniums that bloomed in the most gorgeous shades of blue I'd ever seen in a plant. I had a Japanese anemone that was a whirligig of white flowers until a bunch of blister beetles ate it up. The jerks. Sea thrift, with its little powderpuff flowers growing out of a tuft of grass; Nepeta, or catmint, with its purple flowers. My cat was nuts about catnip, but she had no interest whatsoever in catmint. I planted some dahlia tubers and got some fascinating, gigantic flowers. A perennial hibiscus startled me with magenta flowers as big as dinner plates. Grandma Mary wanted to know what these plants were! And she is wise in all things plant, so that's saying something.

Now, bringing home a bunch of random plants from the nursery doesn't exactly make for an orderly garden. But I didn't care. I loved most the anticipation – of putting this sad, sickly little plant in the ground and giving it good soil and watering it regularly, and generally the plant would perk up and start growing, and the next year it would start flowering, and whoa! So that's what the flowers look like in real life! And it all started with a sad-looking little droopy twig.

That's one of the really cool things about perennials. They can fill a number of roles in the garden. You can get them in a variety of shapes, forms, and colors – whether they're chunky or elegant, variegated, or colorful leaves, sprawling stems or upright, billowing and  carefree or architecturally perfect. Perennials grow in all kinds of conditions, whether it's shade, desert, heat, or cold, and build the background of beautiful borders. Perennials can provide four-season beauty, and they grow stronger by the season. Perennials promise all these things – and they deliver.

At the end of the spring season, when things were slowing down, I was hanging around the garden center one day with my boss and co-worker, just talking. I said, "You know what? I think I'm going to go back to school. And this time, I'm going to major in horticulture. You guys want to come with me?"

"Sure!" they said.

We ended up commuting to school together and took horticulture classes together, and I finally graduated four years later, or close enough. (I minored in writing, naturally.) So, again, perennials turned out to be very helpful. I did my senior thesis on English gardens and totally snowed my Senior Studies professor. He was an Ag man who didn't know much about gardening, so I got an A.

Shortly thereafter, I got a job as city horticulturist. I had a million gardens to plant in the spring. I planted annuals everywhere, but boy, that repetitive motion really hurt my hands and wrists. I used a trowel. Then I tried using bulb planters, which were not effective in the clayey soils in city gardens. Finally I used a little child's shovel to dig a series of holes, then dropped the annuals in and covered them up, in order to save my hands and wrists from all that digging. But this was a lot of labor in spring, and I was always so far behind on all the tasks that needed tending to.

So that fall, I bought a bunch of cheap perennials (everything goes on sale in the fall), wrote down the colors and blooming times for them so I could sort out what would look best where, and then I put them in various gardens to fill out the borders. A one-time planting saved a lot of time and trouble in the spring. Once the perennials filled out and started doing their thing, I didn't have to plant so many annuals, which eased my workload. Now I could do all the other things that needed done, which I couldn't do before because I had been planting annuals.

Oh, and I was a one-woman crew for the whole city. I was assigned inmate labor, but I couldn't send them off by themselves to work on other gardens – too bad. Or I'd get somebody doing community service, which was more of a babysitting job – decidedly unhelpful! At least in the summer I had a very helpful seasonal worker, and how I wish I could have had her working with me in early spring and early fall. But you can't have everything, I suppose.

I had perennials going in everywhere, even in the rose garden, for extra color and to give me an easier time in general. The nice thing was, in fall I could divide the perennials, then plant them out and have many more perennials. I could gather the seeds in October and November, when I was cleaning up the gardens, and plant them in the greenhouse to spread around the parks next spring. Your taxpayer dollars at work.

Anyway, this is why I am such a big fan of perennials. In recent years, roses have pretty much eclipsed perennials for me, These days, I'm starting to come back around to perennials again. They're easy to take care of, they offer a multitude of forms and shapes and sizes and colors and blooming times, and once they're in the ground, they're pretty good about growing for a long time. They got me into my major in college (finally), they saved me a lot of time as a horticulturist, and they look good. All in all, a very, very helpful kind of plant to have.

This book will show you around this fascinating world of perennials. I'll show you how to figure out what you need in your garden by looking at what your garden has to offer your plants in terms of site, the amount of sunlight and rain it gets, and ways to improve the soil for best results. I'll talk about garden design (because with perennials, you work with not only color, but coordinating bloom times for all-season color), how to care for your perennials, how to keep them looking good through the year, and ways to troubleshoot your garden problems, whether it's insect pests, diseases, animals, or weeds.

Welcome aboard!

Hey, if you have any ideas for future books, or see something I've missed in this book that you'd like to see covered, drop me a line at rosefiend@gmail.com and I'll get right on it. Also, if you want to subscribe to my newsletter, go to my website at melindacordell.com and sign up, and you'll always know when my next book will be coming out. You can also help me choose upcoming topics, book covers, etc., and I'll give you free chapters, book samples, and gardening tips. Enjoy!

Perennial Classics is available as an ebook here!

*Me in 1995, when I embarked upon the grand adventure
of being a published author.
I was kind of a writing hotshot back then.
If you want to be perfectly honest, I still am.*

ABOUT THE AUTHOR

I've worked in most all aspects of horticulture – garden centers, wholesale greenhouses, as a landscape designer, and finally as city horticulturist, where I took care of 20+ gardens around the city. I live in northwest Missouri with my husband and kids, the best little family that ever walked the earth. In 2012, when I was hugely pregnant, I graduated from Hamline University with a master's of writing for children; three weeks later, I had a son. It was quite a time.

My first book, **Courageous Women of the Civil War: Soldiers, Spies, Medics, and More** was published by Chicago Review Press in August 2016. This is a series of profiles of women who fought or cared for the wounded during the Civil War.

I've been sending novels out to publishers and agents since 1995, and have racked up I don't know how many hundreds of rejections. I kept getting very close – but not close enough. Agents kept saying, "You're a very good writer, you have an excellent grasp of craft, but I just don't feel that 'spark'...." Even after *Courageous Women* was published, they still weren't interested in my books.

In September 2016, I rage-quit traditional publishing and started self-publishing, because I wanted to get my books out to people who *would* feel that 'spark.' In my first year, I published 15 books. This year I plan to repeat that. (When you've been writing novels for over 20 years, you're going to have a bit of a backlog.) I am working my way completely through it and having a complete blast. I love doing cover work and designing the book interiors. I work full-time as a proofreader, so I handle that in my books as well.

And now I'm finding fans of my books who do feel that 'spark.' They're peaches, every one of them.

I'm finally doing what I was put on this earth to do.

There's no better feeling than that.

If you like this book, please leave a review on my BookBub or Goodreads page. Reviews help me get more readers.

Thanks so much for reading!

melindacordell.com

CPSIA information can be obtained
at www.ICGtesting.com
Printed in the USA
LVHW110844180121
676771LV00006B/355

9 781953 196408